How to
Handle
Adversity

Also by Charles Stanley, available in
Large Print from Walker and Company

The Wonderful Spirit-Filled Life

The Source of My Strength

A Touch of His Freedom

A Touch of His Wisdom

Charles Stanley

How to Handle Adversity

Walker and Company
New York

First Large Print edition published in the United States of America in 1999 by Walker Publishing Company, Inc.

Published simultaneously in Canada by Fitzhenry and Whiteside, Markham, Ontario L3R 4T8

Scripture quotations are from the New American Standard Bible, © 1960, 1962, 1963, 1968, 1971, 1972, 1973, 1975, 1977 by The Lockman Foundation. Used by permission.

Scripture quotations noted NKJV are from THE NEW KING JAMES VERSION. Copyright © 1979, 1980, 1982, Thomas Nelson, Inc., Publishers.

Scripture quotations noted NIV are taken from the HOLY BIBLE: NEW INTERNATIONAL VERSION. Copyright © 1973, 1978, 1984 by the International Bible Society. Used by permission of Zondervan Bible Publishers.

Library of Congress Cataloging-in-Publication Data
Stanley, Charles F.
    How to handle adversity / Charles Stanley. — 1st large print ed.
        p.   cm.
    Originally published: Nashville : Oliver-Nelson, c 1989.
    ISBN 0-8027-2738-7 (lg. print : pbk.)
    1. Consolation. 2. Christian life. 3. Large type books.
I. Title.
[BV4905.2.S63   1999]
248.8'6—dc21   95-50491
                                  CIP

Printed in Canada
10 9 8 7 6 5 4 3 2 1

To Mrs. Ralph Sauls
My steadfast inspiration
in a time of great adversity

I want to thank my son, Andy,
for his insight and assistance
in research and editing.

Contents

How to Handle Adversity

I

Adversity:
Who Is Behind It All?

As Jesus and His disciples passed through Jerusalem, they came upon a man who had been blind from birth. This surfaced a question in the minds of the disciples that they must have been wrestling with for some time. They asked,

> Who sinned, this man or his parents,
> that he should be born blind?
> —John 9:2

Their dilemma was based upon a wrong assumption they had been taught all their lives, namely, that illness is a sign of God's judgment. There was no question in their minds that someone had sinned. But who?

The disciples were trying from their limited perspective to answer a question we often find ourselves asking. It is the "why" question. Why did this happen? Why did my son run away? Why did my father contract cancer? Why did our house burn? Why did I lose my job? Why was I sued?

The questions are endless. Each of us has a specific list. Sometimes there is so much emotion involved we dare not even allow ourselves to verbalize the frustration we feel because asking for and finding no clear-cut answer threatens the foundation of all we believe about God and His goodness. And yet, the questions still linger.

Like the disciples, we are prone to view adversity narrowly. We turn on ourselves and begin an often fruitless journey into our recent—and sometimes not-so-recent—past. Our purpose is to find the reason for the adversity we face. The thought may arise: Surely this is God's way of paying me back. If, however, we are convinced that nothing we have done merits the magnitude of our adversity, we have no choice, it seems, but to question the goodness and faithfulness of God.

2

In His response to the disciples' question, Jesus revealed yet another error that plagued the theology of the day. But His answer did much more than that. It enlightens us and offers a much broader perspective on suffering than that held by many. His answer brings hope to those who have thus far been afraid to ask "why." It allows us to look beyond ourselves—and that is always an improvement!

Jesus answered, "It was neither that this man sinned, nor his parents." In others words, "Your thinking is too narrow. You need some new categories." I believe many well-meaning Christians need some new categories when it comes to the subject of adversity. Thinking too narrowly on this subject sets one up for needless guilt. And as in the case of Jesus' disciples, it warps one's perspective on the suffering of others.

Jesus said,

> It was neither that this man sinned, nor his parents; but it was in order that the works of God might be displayed in him.　　　　　—John 9:3

The implications of that statement are staggering. The phrase "in order that" de-

Is it
possible that
adversity
can originate
with God?

notes purpose. There was a purpose to this man's blindness. The disciples saw his blindness as the result of something. In fact, they saw all illness in terms of result. Jesus, however, let it be known in no uncertain terms that this blindness was not the result of something the man did. This man's blindness was a part of God's purpose. In other words, this man's blindness was from God. That was a difficult sentence to write—much less believe.

Is it possible that adversity can originate with God? All of us would be more comfortable if Jesus had said, "This man is blind because he sinned, but God is going to use it anyway." That would be a much easier pill to swallow. But Jesus leaves us no escape. Sin was not the direct cause of this man's blindness; God was.

A Case in Point

I am aware that such a statement flies in the face of the prosperity theology so prevalent today Yet, a statement such as this one in the gospel of John makes it perfectly clear that God is the engineer of some adversity. We cannot let our theological biases (which we all have) interfere with the clear teaching of Scripture. Fortunately for us, this blind man is not the only scriptural example of God's engineering adversity. In 2 Corinthians 12 the apostle Paul describes his struggle with adversity. He clearly identifies God as the engineer behind his suffering:

> And because of the surpassing greatness of the revelations, for this reason, **to keep me from exalting myself,** there was given me a thorn in the flesh, a messenger of Satan to buffet me—**to keep me from exalting myself!**
> —2 Corinthians 12:7 (emphasis mine)

One might argue, "But it says it was a messenger of Satan." Right! But notice the purpose of Paul's adversity: "To keep me from exalting myself." Do you think Satan would engineer a plan to keep Paul from exalting himself? Of course not. Satan's goal is to cause us to exalt ourselves. He is certainly not going to work against his own destructive purposes. So how does all this fit together? It would seem that God wanted to cause Paul some pain in order to keep him humble. To accomplish this, God sent a messenger of Satan into Paul's life. What exactly this was, we do not know. One thing is certain, however; the idea originated with God. It was His plan, and He used His resources to carry it out.

As difficult as it may be to grasp, the Bible depicts God as the instigator of some adversity. In the remaining chapters we are going to expand upon the relationship between God and adversity. I realize that for some people I have raised many more questions than I have answered. That is all right, as long as you keep reading!

Our Own Doing

God is not the only source of adversity. Oftentimes adversity comes as a result of our own doing. Jesus' disciples were not completely off base in their approach to discerning the cause behind the man's blindness. Adversity is in many cases the result of sin. In fact, sin always results in adversity of some kind. James writes,

> But each one is tempted when he is carried away and enticed by his own lust. Then when lust has conceived, it gives birth to sin; and when sin is accomplished, it brings forth death.
> —James 1:14–15

Sin always results in some form of death. Sometimes it is physical death, but usually it is more subtle. Sin causes our relationships to die. It causes our self-esteem to die. Certain sins kill ambition and discipline. All of these forms of death result in adversity to some degree.

The classic case would be the story of Adam and Eve. Their lives were free of adversity. There was no sickness, death, decay, or suffering of any kind in the Garden of Eden. There was no tension in their relationship with each other. Neither was there any conflict between them and the environment. They could not have wished for anything more. We are not sure how long Adam and Eve lived in the Garden of Eden. We are certain, though, about why they had to leave—sin.

After they disobeyed God by eating of the forbidden fruit, everything changed. Eve would experience pain in childbirth. There would be the potential for conflict between the man and the woman. There would even be conflict between man and his environment. To top it all off, man would have to experience death and thus live his life under the shadow of that monumental foe. Death brought with it fear, sorrow, doubt, and insecurity. All of these were the result of sin. From that moment on, life for Adam and Eve would be full of adversity—and all because of sin.

The Roots of Evil

This biblical narrative does more than simply illustrate the possible connection between sin and adversity. It serves as the foundation for answering many of life's toughest questions. It is clear from even a cursory reading of these first few chapters that God never intended for man to experience the adversity and sorrow brought about by our forefather's sin. Death was not a part of God's original plan for man. Death is an interruption. It is God's enemy as well as man's. It is the opposite of all He desired to accomplish.

Sickness and pain are certainly no friends of God. There was no sickness in the Garden of Eden. It was not a part of God's original plan for man. The ministry of Christ bears witness to this truth. Everywhere He went He healed the sick. God shares our disdain for disease. Sickness is an intruder. It had no place in God's world in the beginning; it will have no place in His world in the end.

Death, disease, famine, earthquakes, war—
these things were not part of God's original
plan. Yet they are part of our reality. Why?
Did God lose His grip? Has He abandoned
us? Is He no longer a good God? No. Our
reality has been fashioned by Adam's choice
to sin. And sin always results in adversity.

God's goodness and power are not to be
measured in the balance of the tragedy and
adversity we experience day in and day out.
If His goodness is to be questioned, let it
be done in light of His original purpose as
well as His ultimate plan.

> And I heard a loud voice from the
> throne, saying, "Behold the tabernacle
> of God is among men, and He shall
> dwell among them, and they shall be
> His people, and God Himself shall be
> among them, and He shall wipe away
> every tear from their eyes; and there
> shall no longer be any death; there
> shall no longer be any mourning, or
> crying, or pain; the first things have
> passed away."
> —Revelation 21:3–4

It is God who will wipe away every tear.
It is God who will do away with death, cry-

ing, pain, and sorrow. Why will He do these things? Because He is a good and faithful God. How can He do such things? By the strength of His might. He is the all-powerful Sovereign of the universe. Nothing is too hard for Him.

A Living Example

The idea that adversity is sometimes the result of sin hardly needs biblical support. Each of us could give testimony to this principle. Every speeding ticket or fine we have ever paid serves as evidence. The last argument you had with your spouse, parent, or child probably stemmed from sin in some form or another. The sorrow and pain caused by a divorce or even separation are always related in some way to sin. Sometimes it is personal sin that brings adversity into our lives. On other occasions the sin of someone else causes us difficulty. Jesus' disciples were not completely wrong; adversity and sin do go hand in hand.

As self-evident as this may seem, it is amazing how we sometimes cannot see, or refuse to see, the relationship. Recently a mother brought her teenage son to see me. The problem, as she saw it, was her son's involvement with "the wrong crowd." She went on to explain how her son's interaction with this group had caused him to develop a bad attitude toward authority. As a result, he had become impossible to live with.

After several meetings, the truth finally surfaced. The situation was one in which the boy's mother had left her husband (the boy's father), and she was completely unwilling to work toward reconciling the relationship. The boy wanted to live with his father, but his mother would not hear of it. I talked with the father on several occasions. He took responsibility for his part in the conflicts at home. He was willing to do whatever he had to do to get his family back together. His wife, on the other hand, would not budge.

When I explained to the woman how a hostile separation usually affects the children involved, she became angry. "I told you why he is acting the way he is," she said. "It's his friends." Nothing I said made any difference. She could not (or would not) see any connection between her son's behavior at home and her response to her husband. As far as she was concerned, the problem was her son's. On several occasions she was willing to publicly request prayer for herself in regard to the sorrow her son was causing her. But she never came to grips with the fact that the conflict she was experiencing with her son was directly related to her own sin.

It is hard to put a percentage on this, but I would guess that 60 to 70 percent of the people I counsel are suffering from the consequences of their own sin or the sin of another. Some of the most difficult counseling situations I deal with are those in which an innocent party is suffering from the disobedience of another. It always seems so unjust. Yet part of coping with that type of adversity is realizing its source—sin. I admit that this is not a very satisfying answer in some cases. One reason is that if I am suffering because of someone else's sin, there is really nothing I can do about it, except suffer! If it is my sin I am suffering from, I can at least take some consolation in the fact that if I had not erred in some way, I would not be suffering. But when it is truly someone else's fault, the situation can be extremely frustrating.

Later on we will discuss how to respond to different types of adversity. The point I am making here is that sometimes there is no explanation for adversity other than the fact that we are feeling the effects of someone's sin.

The Adversary Himself

There is a third source of adversity: Satan. In one sense he is ultimately behind all adversity. He is directly responsible for Adam and Eve's being led astray and, therefore, for the calamity that followed. However, his involvement in adversity extends far beyond his activity in the Garden of Eden. He is alive and active today.

Several biblical accounts illustrate Satan's role in adversity. The clearest example is the story of Job. Those who attribute all adversity to sin of some kind or a lack of faith have a difficult time with this narrative. They attribute Job's problems to his pride or the sin of his children. But the writer puts those theories to rest in the first verse of the book.

> There was a man in the land of Uz, whose name was Job, and that man was **blameless, upright, fearing God, and turning away from evil.**
> —Job 1:1 (emphasis mine)

Later in the same chapter God Himself gives His evaluation of Job.

And the LORD said to Satan, "Have you considered My servant Job? For there is no one like him on the earth, a blameless and upright man, fearing God and turning away from evil."

—Job 1:8

There can be no doubt about it. Job was a righteous man. The adversity he faced was not the result of pride. The ensuing discussion between God and Satan spells out exactly why Job suffered the way he did.

Then Satan answered the LORD, "Does Job fear God for nothing? Hast Thou not made a hedge about him and his house and all that he has, on every side? Thou hast blessed the work of his hands, and his possessions have increased in the land. But put forth Thy hand now and touch all that he has; he will surely curse Thee to Thy face." Then the LORD said to Satan, "Behold, all that he has is in your power, only do not put forth your hand on him." So Satan departed from the presence of the LORD.

—Job 1:9–12

So Satan sets out to destroy all Job has. Yet Job continues to serve God and walk in His ways. So Satan makes another request of God.

> And Satan answered the LORD and said, "Skin for skin! Yes, all that a man has he will give for his life. However, put forth Thy hand, now, and touch his bone and his flesh; he will curse Thee to Thy face." So the LORD said to Satan, "Behold, he is in your power, only spare his life." Then Satan went out from the presence of the LORD, and smote Job with sore boils from the sole of his foot to the crown of his head.
>
> —Job 2:4–7

Job's adversity was from Satan. The writer makes a clear distinction in this book. Satan dares God to send adversity into Job's life. But God in turn instructs Satan to do the dirty work. Permission came from God. The adversity came from Satan.

Peter tells us that Satan is roaming around like a lion seeking those whom he can destroy through adversity. He writes,

> Be of sober spirit, be on the alert. Your adversary, the devil, prowls about like a roaring lion, seeking someone to devour. But resist him, firm in your faith, knowing that the same experiences of suffering are being accomplished by your brethren who are in the world.   —1 Peter 5:8–9

Oftentimes this passage is used to talk about Satan's involvement in our temptations. The real context, however, is that of suffering. Satan roams around looking for ways to bring adversity into our lives. He wants us to suffer, for suffering often destroys one's faith in God. Peter instructs these believers to be on the alert so that in the midst of their suffering they will not lose sight of who is causing it as well as how God is going to use it.

How Do We Know?

In our day-to-day experience it is sometimes difficult to determine the source of our adversity. Adversity related to our personal sin is usually easy to identify. Beyond that, though, things begin to run together. We certainly do not want to rebuke the devil for something God is behind. Neither do we want to just grin and bear it if there is something we can do to put an end to our suffering.

The Bible does not give us three simple steps to aid us in determining the source of our adversity. This used to really bother me. For a long time, when I faced adversity, I would pray and pray for God to give me some indication as to why I was suffering. Then I realized why those kinds of prayers rarely seemed to be answered. There was and is a much more important issue at stake.

Far more important than the source of adversity is the response to adversity Why? Because adversity, regardless of the source, is God's most effective tool for deepening your faith and commitment to Him. The areas in which you are experiencing the most adversity are the areas in which God is at work. When someone says, "God is not doing anything in my life," my response is always, "So then, you don't have any problems?" Why? Because the best way to identify God's involvement in your life is to consider your response to adversity. God uses adversity, regardless of the source. But your response to adversity determines whether or not God is able to use it to accomplish His purpose. In fact, adversity can destroy your faith. If you do not respond correctly, adversity can put you into a spiritual tailspin from which you may never recover. It all hinges on your response.

As much as we all want to know the answer to the "why" question, it is really not the most significant question. The real question each of us needs to ask is, "How should I respond?" To spend too much time trying to answer the "why" question is to run the risk of missing what God wants to teach us. Ironically enough, concentrating on why often hinders us from ever discovering why. If it is in God's sovereign will to reveal to us, this side of eternity, the answer to that question, it will be as we respond correctly.

One of the greatest struggles of my life surrounded my decision to move from Bartow, Florida, to Atlanta. Bartow is a small town in central Florida. Our home was in walking distance of three lakes. The neighborhood was safe. We knew all of our neighbors. Bartow seemed like the perfect environment in which to raise our children. To complicate things even further, we had only lived there about one year when a friend of mine approached me about moving to Atlanta to be the associate pastor at First Baptist

Church. I thanked him for his vote of confidence but made it clear that I was not at all interested.

A few weeks later a pulpit committee showed up to hear me preach. Once again, I was polite, but I told them I was not interested. They asked me to pray about it. I told them I would. What else could I say? So one evening my wife, Anna, and I began praying about whether or not it was God's will for us to move to Atlanta. The strangest thing happened. The more we prayed, the more both of us became convinced we should go. When we would talk about it, it did not make any sense at all. Why would God want me to become an associate pastor when I had already been the senior pastor for three churches? Why would God move us after being in Bartow only thirteen months? Why would a good God want me to move my family to a place like Atlanta?

Two months later we moved. And about two years after that, I understood why. My point is this: oftentimes, the explanations we are so desperately seeking will become clear as we respond properly to adversity.

Surely the disciples stood at Calvary wondering why such a thing was allowed to take place. Humanly speaking, it made no sense at all. But in a few days all the pieces fit together. Oftentimes we stand like the disciples at Calvary. We watch our hopes and dreams shatter before our eyes. We see our loved ones suffer. We see family members die. And like the disciples, we wonder why.

We must remember that Christ's death, burial, and resurrection serve as the context of all our suffering. God, through those events, took the greatest tragedy in the history of the world and used it to accomplish His greatest triumph—the salvation of man. If the murder of the perfect Son of God can be explained, how much more can we trust that God is accomplishing His purposes through the adversity we face every day?

The source of our adversity is not to be our primary concern. Think about it. What was the source of the adversity Christ faced? Sin, Satan, or God? Actually, all three were involved. Yet Christ's response allowed our heavenly Father to take this tragedy and use it for the greatest good. That is the pattern. That is God's goal for us through all the adversities of life.

Have you been so hung up on trying to figure out why adversity has come your way that perhaps you have missed God? Has the adversity in your life strengthened your faith, or has it weakened your faith? Adversity is a reality that none of us can avoid. Therefore, it is in your best interest to begin responding in such a way that the negative can be used to accomplish the will of God in your life. And as you begin responding correctly, perhaps you will begin to understand why!

2

The Power of Perspective

As I write this chapter, one of my good friends is watching his wife die of cancer. The doctors have given up hope. We have prayed and prayed, and yet there seems to be no sign of God's healing hand. Jim sits by his wife's side all day, every day. Anything he can do to make his wife more comfortable, he does gladly. And yet he remains powerless to do the one thing he desires most of all—heal his wife.

I have heard Jim pray. I have seen him hurt. His faith has not been shattered; but it has been dealt a severe blow. He will recover. But the question will always remain:

Why did this happen? What was the point? What was accomplished? Why the grief so unfairly imposed upon such a God-fearing family?

Jim and his family are certainly not the first persons to ask such painful and complex questions. And they are well aware of that. In anticipation of questions raised by circumstances such as these, God has given us in the gospel of John a narrative that helps us gain the perspective needed to survive tragedies such as that faced by Jim.

The problem with studying any familiar passage is that we rarely allow ourselves to feel what the characters must have felt. Why should we? We usually know what happens in the end. Unfortunately, this familiarity with the Scriptures often robs us of their intended results. It is hard to feel the fear David must have felt when he faced Goliath when we know from the outset that he comes out the victor. We miss the sense of isolation Moses must have felt as he fled Egypt for his life. After all, he ends up a hero. So as you approach this familiar narrative in John 11, try to forget the end of the story. Do your best to put yourself in the shoes, or maybe the sandals, of the people involved. If you read what happens but neglect to consider what must have been felt, you lose some of the richest insights of this story.

"He Whom You Love Is Sick"

> Now a certain man was sick, Lazarus of Bethany, the village of Mary and her sister Martha. And it was the Mary who anointed the Lord with ointment, and wiped His feet with her hair, whose brother Lazarus was sick. The sisters therefore sent to Him, saying, "Lord, behold he whom You love is sick." —John 11:1–3

The household of Mary and Martha is one in which Jesus and His disciples had been given hospitality whenever they had been in the area of Judea. Apparently, Lazarus was a wealthy man, and he used his wealth to support the ministry of Christ. The fact that Mary and Martha sent for Jesus as soon as Lazarus became ill is evidence of their faith in His power. No doubt they thought, If Jesus is willing to heal total strangers, certainly He will jump at the opportunity to heal one who has been a friend. But such was not the case.

But when Jesus heard it, He said, "This sickness is not unto death, but for the glory of God, that the Son of God may be glorified by it." Now Jesus loved Martha, and her sister, and Lazarus. When therefore He heard that he was sick, He stayed then two days longer in the place where He was.

—John 11:4–6

These verses make absolutely no sense, humanly speaking. That is why I love this story, because most adversity makes about as much sense from our perspective. It is obviously stated that Jesus loves this family; then He makes no move to relieve their suffering. I can relate to that. Whenever the bottom drops out, I go scrambling for the verses in the Bible that remind me of God's love—yet at times it seems God is unwilling to follow through with any action.

We need to pause here because at this point in the narrative we have our greatest struggles. I am referring to that time between the point we ask God for help and the point at which He does something. It is so easy to read, "He stayed then two days longer." But the delay was like an eternity for Mary and Martha. The Scripture informs us that they knew the general area in which Jesus was ministering at the time. They also knew about how long it would take Him to make the trip to Bethany. So they waited. And as the hours dragged on, they watched their brother grow weaker and weaker.

Finally the day arrived when, according to the normal traveling time, Jesus should arrive. No doubt they took turns sitting with Lazarus. That way one of them could go out to the road to look for Jesus. I can imagine Mary or Martha asking all the men and women coming from the direction of Perea if they had seen a group of twelve or so men headed that way. As they would shake their heads no, the sisters' hope burned a little lower. "Why didn't He come? Maybe He never got the message? Maybe He left Perea without sending word back to us? Where is He? After all we have done for Him, it is the least He could do." And yet He failed to come when they expected Him.

Lazarus died. Maybe Mary came in early one morning to check on him and found him dead. Perhaps it was in the afternoon when both Mary and Martha were at his side that he breathed his last breath. Whatever the situation, both women felt that hollow, helpless feeling that always accompanies death.

It was over. He was gone. Soon their thoughts turned to Jesus—Why didn't He come? How could He know what we were going through and yet stay away?

These, no doubt, are some of the questions you have asked as you have cried out to God in the midst of the adversity in your life. How can a God of love stand back and watch my friend and his wife suffer and not do anything about it? How can He watch from the balcony of heaven as women are physically or sexually abused? How can He watch husbands walk out on their wives and children? Does He know what is going on down here?

Once again, this narrative is helpful. Jesus knew exactly what was going on. He knew what Mary and Martha were going through. He knew his friend's condition was worsening. And He knew the moment Lazarus died.

> And after that He said to them [the disciples], "Our friend Lazarus has fallen asleep." —John 11: 11

Yet He did nothing! Keep in mind, Lazarus was not some guy off the street. He had invited Jesus into his home. Lazarus had expressed faith in Christ and His ministry. He was a good man. He certainly had more faith than most of the other people Jesus had healed. Some of them did not even know who Christ was (see John 9). But Jesus was nowhere to be found when Lazarus needed Him most.

To add insult to injury, Jesus had the nerve to say to His disciples,

> Lazarus is dead, and **I am glad** for your sakes that I was not there.
> —John 11: 14–15 (emphasis mine)

Jesus was "glad"? How could He say such a thing? Two of his best friends go through emotional turmoil; another friend dies of an illness; and Jesus says He is glad? What could He have possibly been thinking? What was going through His mind?

My friend, the answer to that question is the key to unlocking the mystery of tragedy in this life. To understand what was going on in the mind of Christ and in the economy of God in a situation like this one is to discover the universal principle that puts together and holds together all of life—both now and for eternity. Christ had a goal in all of this, a goal so important that it was worth the emotional agony Mary and Martha had to endure. It was worth risking the destruction of their faith. It was even worth the death of a faithful friend. What Jesus, in conjunction with His heavenly Father, had in mind was so incredible that even through the pain surrounding the whole event Jesus could say, "I am glad this has happened." In other words, "Men, what you are about to see is so fantastic that it is worth the pain and death of my beloved friend." If they were like us, they probably thought, What could be worth all of this?

"If You Had Been Here"

Now Bethany was near Jerusalem, about two miles off; and many of the Jews had come to Martha and Mary, to console them concerning their brother. Martha therefore, when she heard that Jesus was coming, went to meet Him; but Mary still sat in the house. Martha therefore said to Jesus, "Lord, if You had been here, my brother would not have died." . . .

And when she had said this, she went away, and called Mary her sister, saying secretly, "The Teacher is here, and is calling for you." And when she heard it she arose quickly, and was coming to Him. . . .

Therefore, when Mary came where Jesus was, she saw Him, and fell at His feet, saying to Him, "Lord, if You had been here, my brother would not have died."
—John 11:18–21, 28–29, 32

Mary and Martha, for all their time spent with the Son of God, were still human to the core. They wanted to know one thing: "Jesus, where in the world have You been?" They had no doubt that Jesus could have healed their brother; Martha even indicates that she believes there is still hope (see John 11:22). But the fact that He had seemingly ignored their plight had left them confused and frustrated. Why did He delay?

When Jesus therefore saw her weeping, and the Jews who came with her, also weeping, He was deeply moved in spirit, and was troubled, and said, "Where have you laid him?" They said to Him, "Lord, come and see." Jesus wept. And so the Jews were saying, "Behold how He loved him!"
—John 11:33–36

At this juncture any doubt about Jesus' love and concern for Lazarus is laid to rest. "Jesus wept." Yet His overt concern about His friend Lazarus adds another layer of mystery to the story. If Jesus was so concerned, why did He not come to Lazarus's aid? Why did He let him die?

Once again we are faced with what appears to be an unsolvable mystery. It becomes apparent that whatever Christ had in mind, whatever He was trying to accomplish, it was worth sacrificing the emotions of the ones He loved as well as His own. Jesus wept when He arrived to find Lazarus dead. Think about it. His knowledge of the future did not keep Him from identifying with the sorrow of those around Him.

Asking the Right Questions

If anything is clear from this story, it is that some things are so important to God that they are worth interrupting the happiness and health of His children in order to accomplish them. That is an awesome thought. To some, it may seem like an indictment of the character of God. But this principle will become clearer through the pages and chapters that follow. Whether some persons can fit this idea into their theology or not, the fact remains that the Son of God allowed those He loved to suffer and die for the sake of some higher purpose.

Some individuals may think such a statement implies that we are merely pawns to be moved about and even abused at God's whims. But remember, "Jesus wept." He was moved with emotion at the sight of Mary and Martha's sorrow. He was touched by the love they had for their brother. He was not emotionally isolated from the pain suffered by those whose perspective was different from His own.

When you hurt, God hurts. Regardless of what He may be in the process of accomplishing, regardless of how noble His purposes may be, He is in touch with what you are feeling. He is not like the football coach who sneers at his players when they complain of their pain. He is not like the boxing coach who whispers into his fighter's ear, "No pain, no gain." Nor is he like the parent who laughs and says to a child who has lost a first love, "Don't worry. You'll get over it."

Through all the pain and adversity God may allow us to face, two things are always true. First, He is sensitive to what we are feeling:

> For we do not have a high priest who
> cannot sympathize with our weak-
> nesses.   —Hebrews 4:15

Jesus wept over Lazarus. He weeps over our sorrow as well.

Second, whatever He is in the process of accomplishing through our suffering will always be for our best interest. The degree to which things actually work out for our best interest is determined by our response. As we trust God through our adversity, when all is said and done, we will sincerely believe it was worth it all.

"How?" you might ask. "How could what I am going through at home work out for my best interest? How could God ever use the death of my spouse (or child)? What could possibly be worth the isolation and hurt I am feeling now?"

When I was a little boy, I used to ask some of those same questions. My father died when I was seven months old, so I grew up without a dad. I remember watching my friends with their fathers and wondering why I couldn't have one, too. It didn't make any sense. My mom had to work long, hard hours in a textile mill. By the time I got up in the morning to go to school, she was already at work. I had to learn to fix my own breakfast and dress myself for school by the time I was six years old.

By the grace of God, my response to all of that was different from that of many young men who lose their fathers. Instead of rebelling against God for taking my dad, I decided at a very young age that I would look to Him to be my Father. My dad's death did not cause me to turn away from God; rather, I turned toward Him. I learned early in life about the daily sufficiency of Christ. I learned how to pray. I learned how to walk by faith. The untimely death of my father was actually the catalyst God used to teach me the most important lessons of life—the lessons that have allowed me to survive intense rejection as an adult on both a professional level and a personal level. But at the age of seven or eight I could not see what God was up to. It made no sense at all then. There was nothing to compensate for the loneliness I felt. In fact, it has taken me over forty years to make sense out of the adversity I faced as a child. And the lessons continue.

Not too long ago, my son, Andy, said to me, "You know, Dad, Becky and I probably reaped the real benefits of your not having a father when you grew up."

"What do you mean?" I asked.

"Well," he said, "when it came time to raise your own kids, you didn't have a pattern to follow. You had to be completely dependent upon the Lord for everything."

As I thought about it, he was right. And when I realized how committed they are to the Lord, when I thought about how different they are from many preachers' children, I was even able to thank the Lord for not giving me a father. If that was what it took to prepare me to raise my own children, it was worth it all!

A Sickness Not Unto Death

What, then, did Jesus have in mind by delaying His return to Bethany, thus allowing Lazarus to die? What was so important that He was willing to allow His close friends to go through the agony of watching their brother die. The answer to that question gives us a great deal of insight into the character and economy of God. Jesus Himself provided the answer when He was first informed of Lazarus's illness and then again when He stood at the tomb.

The sisters therefore sent to Him, saying, "Lord, behold, he whom You love is sick." But when Jesus heard it, He said, **"This sickness is not unto death, but for the glory of God, that the Son of God may be glorified by it**." Now Jesus loved Martha, and her sister, and Lazarus.

—John 11:3–5 (emphasis mine)

And so they removed the stone. And Jesus raised His eyes, and said, "Father, I thank Thee that Thou heardest Me. And I knew that Thou hearest Me always; but because of the people standing around I said it, **that they may believe that Thou didst send Me**."

—John 11:41–42 (emphasis mine)

From the very beginning, Jesus had two specific purposes in mind. His purpose was not to cause Lazarus to die. Neither was it to cause Mary and her sister mental and emotional anguish. On the contrary, His goals in all that happened were to bring glory to God and to cause others to believe in Him. The opportunity to accomplish these two things was worth the pain and suffering Mary,

Martha, and Lazarus had to experience. To Christ, this opportunity to publicly display the power of God was worth risking the rejection of some of His closest friends. It was even worth the death of a loved one.

But for the Glory of God

To glorify something is to so arrange things as to focus attention on it or bring it honor. We glorify a picture when we hang it at a focal point in a room. We may further glorify it by shining a light on it. We glorify a singer when we put him or her on a stage and focus our attention on the performance. When we stand and applaud at the end, we are, again, glorifying the performer.

Jesus said that the purpose of this seeming tragedy was the glorification of Him and His Father. Lazarus died so that for a short moment in time the focus of attention might be God and His Son. Jesus was so given over to seeing His heavenly Father glorified that He was "glad" Lazarus died if that was what it took. This was not out of character for our Savior. He spent his whole life in an attempt to focus the attention of man on His Father. He did everything with that purpose in mind.

At the end of His earthly ministry He summed up His life's work by saying,

> I have glorified Thee on the earth, having accomplished the work which Thou hast given Me to do.
>
> —John 17:4

As much as Jesus dreaded the cross, He knew that His own death was a part of His Father's plan to draw attention to Himself. Yet knowledge of what He would accomplish through His death and resurrection in no way erased the pain of the cross. Neither did it minimize the emotional anguish of watching His followers abandon Him at the moment He needed them most. When He uttered, "Yet not My will, but Thine be done," He in essence said, "Whatever it takes, regardless of the sacrifice, let it be done!" He then went to the cross determined to bring His Father glory, even at the expense of His own life.

Many Believed in Him

The second purpose behind Jesus' delay was that many might put their trust in Him as the Messiah. More important than keeping everybody healthy was moving people to faith. So Christ purposefully waited until it was too late so that He might perform a miracle of such magnitude that many would put their faith in Him. And that is exactly what happened (see John 11:45). Just as He allowed those He loved to suffer for the sake of those who had not believed, so He will allow us to suffer today. Nothing gets the attention of an unbeliever like a saint who is suffering successfully. It is easy to talk about Christ when everything is going fine. Our words take on a great deal more significance when they are spoken from a life filled with pain.

I can hear the skeptic now, "Are you saying that God would allow me—His child— to suffer for the sake of some unsaved person?" That is exactly what I am saying. But keep in mind, it was His Son who prepared the way. If almighty God saw fit to allow His own Son to suffer unjustly that we might be saved, why should we think it below us to suffer so that others might believe?

The late Dr. Barnhouse had an experience during his ministry that illustrates this point perfectly. He was conducting a week of services in a church. The pastor of the church and his wife were expecting their first child. During the week, Dr. Barnhouse would kid with the pastor about his being so uptight.

On the last night of services the pastor did not show up. Dr. Barnhouse assumed he was at the hospital with his wife, so he went ahead with the service. Toward the end of the service he noticed that the pastor slipped in quietly and took a seat on the back pew. When the service was completed, the pastor made his way to the front, dismissed everyone, and asked Dr. Barnhouse if he could see him in his office.

"Certainly," he said and followed him to the back.

As they shut the door behind them, the pastor wheeled around and blurted out, "Dr. Barnhouse, our child has Down syndrome. I haven't told my wife yet. I don't know what I'm going to tell her."

"Friend, this is of the Lord," Dr. Barnhouse said. And then he turned to this passage in the Old Testament:

> And the LORD said to him [Moses], "Who has made man's mouth? Or who makes him dumb or deaf, or seeing or blind? Is it not I, the LORD?"
> —Exodus 4:11

"Let me see that," the pastor said. He read it again.

As the pastor studied the passage, Dr. Barnhouse said, "My friend, you know the promise in Romans 8. All things work together for good—including this special child—for those who love the Lord."

The pastor closed the Bible. Slowly he walked out of the office and went straight to the hospital room of his wife. When he arrived, she said, "They won't let me see my baby. What's wrong? I've asked to see my baby, and they won't let me."

The young pastor took his wife by the hand and said, "Who has made the dumb or deaf or seeing or blind, is it not I, the Lord? Darling, the Lord has blessed us with a child with Down syndrome."

She cried long and hard. Then as she began to settle down, she said, "Where did you get that?"

"From God's own Word," he said.

"Let me see." Then she read it.

Meanwhile news of the birth swept through the hospital. This information was of special interest to the switchboard operator in the hospital. She was not a Christian. In fact she was a cruel woman who enjoyed seeing Christians crumble. She was convinced that under pressure, there was really no difference between Christians and everybody else. When the pastor's wife called her mother to give her the news, the operator listened in—expecting the young mother to go to pieces.

"Mother, the Lord has blessed us with a child with Down syndrome. We don't know the nature of the blessing, but we do know it is a blessing." There were no tears, no hysteria, no breakdown.

The operator was shocked. But when she absorbed what she heard, she began telling everyone. Soon the entire hospital was buzzing with the story of the pastor and his wife's response. The following Sunday the pastor was back in his pulpit. In the congregation, unknown to him, were the telephone operator and seventy nurses and staff members from the hospital. At the conclusion of the service the pastor offered an invitation.

"If you have never met Jesus Christ, I want to extend to you an invitation to do so."

That morning thirty nurses from the hospital came forward receiving Christ. All because of one special child and the faith of the young pastor and his wife.

Would God allow this child to be born with a handicapping condition for the sake of thirty nurses? Absolutely. Just as He allowed a man to be born blind that His Son might heal him. Just as He would allow one whom He loved to die in order that he might be raised. And just as He allowed His own Son to be murdered in order that many might receive eternal life. God allows suffering so that others might come to faith in His Son.

The Role of Pain

It has been said that where there is no pain, there is no gain. This phrase applies not only in the realm of athletics, but in the spiritual realm as well. The pattern we see in Christ's earthly ministry and in His personal pilgrimage bears this out. Suffering is the means by which God brings glory to Himself and His Son. Although suffering is usually the last thing to be considered useful, it is God's most useful tool. Nothing compares with suffering when it comes to bringing God glory, for nothing else highlights our dependence, weakness, and insecurity like suffering.

But suffering is also the way God brings honor and glory to His children. In his second letter to the Corinthians Paul makes this clear when he writes,

> For momentary, light affliction is pro-
> ducing for us an eternal weight of
> glory far beyond all comparison, while
> we look not at the things which are
> seen, but at the things which are not
> seen; for the things which are seen are
> temporal, but the things which are not
> seen are eternal.
> —2 Corinthians 4:17–18

Adversity in this life, when handled properly, provides for the believer glory and honor
in the life to come. In this passage Paul
speaks of glory as if it were a tangible thing
that could be progressively added to. It is
as if each believer has an eternal account
wherein glory is being applied in relation
to personal suffering on this earth.

He closes this section by giving us the
motivation we need to adopt this perspective. Simply put, our suffering is temporary
— just like the bodies in which we are suffering are temporary. But the rewards we are
accumulating while in these temporary bodies
are eternal. What an investment! What a system! God has allowed us to participate in a
system by which the temporal can be used
to gain what is eternal.

This truth is especially important as we

focus on the end of the story of Lazarus. Many may be tempted to say, "Well, it always works out fine for people in the Bible, but my husband was not raised from the dead." Or "My wife never came back to me." Or "I have not seen God get any glory out of my situation." To which God would add one essential word, "YET!" Remember, eventually, Lazarus died for good. Christ's miracle was in that sense only temporary. The glory connected with Lazarus's being alive was short-lived. Any time God bails us out of adversity—as He often does—the glory connected with that is to some degree temporary. Yet God has established a means by which our suffering can result in eternal glory, glory that exalts not only Him, but also those who suffered.

"Remove the Stone"

> Jesus said, "Remove the stone." Martha, the sister of the deceased, said to Him, "Lord, by this time there will be a stench, for he has been dead four days." Jesus said to her, "Did I not say to you, if you believe, you will see the glory of God?"
>
> —John 11:39–40

Had they refused to remove the stone, they would have suffered for nothing. No good would have come from it. Mary and her sister would have missed the glory of God. I meet people all the time who are dealing with personal tragedy of the worst kind. Sometimes it is their own fault. At other times they are the victims. Oftentimes greater than the tragedy itself is their response. Because they see no immediate good, they assume that there is no good to be found, that God has abandoned them or perhaps was never interested in the first place. They refuse to remove the stone. They will not trust God with what they cannot see.

If God can gain glory for Himself from the unjustified murder of His Son, can we not trust Him to somehow glorify Himself in and through the things we struggle with on a daily basis? If God can find for Himself glory in the death of His Son's close friend, should we not trust Him to do the same through even the major tragedies in our lives? God specializes in taking tragedy and turning it into triumph. The greater the tragedy, the greater the potential for triumph.

There will always be things we cannot explain. In time some answers will become clear, while others will remain a mystery.

One thing we do know, God is in the business of glorifying Himself. He wants the world's attention, and oftentimes adversity is His way of getting it. As Christians, we are His representatives. We are extensions of the ministry of Christ on the earth. We, then, are the tools through which God will attract the world's attention. He works through our conversations, our character, our preaching, and our adversity. His success in all of these areas depends in part upon our response.

"If You Believe, You Will See the Glory of God"

Martha trusted Christ and removed the stone. I believe Jim, too, will trust God to gain glory for Himself through the tragedy of his wife's terminal illness. What about you? Are there stones in your life that are blocking the Lord's ability to gain for Himself the glory that is rightfully His? Have you cut your faith off at the point where things quit making sense? Have you attached your faith only to what can be seen? Have you refused to look beyond your loss? Have you allowed your pain to so consume you that you have forgotten that God may have something He wants to accomplish?

You have only two options. You can trust God to glorify Himself through your adversity. Or you can focus on your loss and spend your time searching for answers. In doing so, you may cause the means by which God was going to do something great to become a tragic end in itself.

An old saint contemplating his life summed up the point of this chapter perfectly:

> And I may return in faded armor
> Full of patches bent and aged.
> And I may face the heat of battle,
> To free the damned and free the slaves.
> And I may know both pain and rejection,
> The betrayal of my friends.
> But the glory that awaits me,
> Will make it worth it in the end—in
> the end.

Friend, regardless of the adversity you are facing, if you trust God, you, too, will one day say, "It was worth it all!"

3

When God Is Silent

One of the most frustrating things about Christianity is that our God is oftentimes so quiet. When I have finished pouring out my heart to the Lord, I would like a little response. Anything would be fine; and yet He is silent. I'm sure you have felt the same frustration. The strange thing is that I am acutely aware of God's silence when I need Him the most. There have been plenty of times, after weeping over a crisis either in my life or in the life of someone I love, that just a word from the Lord would have been comforting—and yet He was silent.

I can think of counseling situations that have left me dumbfounded. So many situations arising today seem to go beyond the bounds of what the Scriptures address. A word from God would have been so timely, so helpful to those involved—and yet He was silent. There are times I wish He would just send an angel to answer a few basic questions for me. I have faced adversities that seemed at the time to be such a waste: children dying, men leaving their godly wives, a close friend suddenly becoming ill. If only the Lord would have appeared and simply said, "I am still in control." Anything would have helped, but He remained silent.

No Comment

To make things even worse, when we read the Bible, it seems as if God was always speaking to the men whose stories fill the pages. When Peter was thrown into prison, an angel appeared to tell him everything was going to be all right. When Abraham got ripped off by Lot, the Lord spoke a word of comfort to him. Paul had some theological questions and was taken up into the third heaven to have a talk with God. It does not seem fair. After all, my faith would be stronger, too, if every time I faced adversity, an angel from God showed up to tell me what to do. But it does not work that way for us. God is incredibly silent sometimes; we receive no comment from Him to help us.

For believers, God's silence makes adversity much more difficult to endure because our worldview includes a loving God who has presented Himself to us as a Father. When tragedy strikes or difficult times overtake us, our worldview comes under attack. The questions reach the surface of our consciousness. We begin to doubt. Then more than ever we need a word from God. Yet, so often, He remains silent.

You may be one of the thousands of singles in this country who is seeking the right spouse. You have done your best to be faithful to your standards. You are committed to waiting for God's best. But nothing is happening. So you have begun to wonder if there is anything to this bit about "waiting on God."

You may have a job or career in which you are very unhappy. You pray and pray and pray, but feel no peace about staying or leaving. You are willing to do the right thing—whatever it is. But God just doesn't seem to be saying anything.

Or maybe you are dealing with the death of a loved one or some other tragedy that

God's silence
is in no way
indicative of
His activity
or involvement
in our lives.

has taken you by surprise. You are doing the best you can to make yourself believe that God has a purpose in it, that He has not abandoned you. But in your heart you wonder: Maybe there is no God, or Maybe He is just not interested in me. Slowly your faith begins to erode. If only God would say something—anything.

Questions . . . Questions . . . Questions

All of this raises two basic questions. First, what in the world is God up to when we are hurting and need to hear from Him so desperately? Second, what are we to do in the meantime? The answers to these questions are indispensable if we are to deal successfully with adversity. As long as we are in a fog about God's whereabouts and His response to our situation, there will always be room for doubt. But reassurance of His involvement alone is not enough. We need direction as well.

The purpose of this chapter is to answer these two questions. By doing so, I pray that God will erase from your heart forever the awful fear that perhaps He is not interested in your hurt, that He has more important things with which to concern Himself.

To answer these questions, we are going to take a look at the life of Joseph. Let me remind you again not to allow your mind to race to the end of these narratives. If you do, you will miss what God is trying to say. When the Bible presents a particular character's life, the author focuses on those events that are relevant to the theme he is following. This gives the impression oftentimes that the lives of these characters were filled with one supernatural event after another. But that is not the case at all. There were weeks, months, and even years in which nothing special seemed to happen. As we study this Old Testament story, put yourself in the place of the character. Like us, Joseph was forced to deal with the silence of God in the midst of grave adversity.

Just When He Needed Him Most

Joseph's troubles started as a teenager. At seventeen he was his father's favorite, and that did not go over well with his ten older brothers. They were jealous, and their jealousy turned to hatred (see Gen. 37:4). If that was not enough, Joseph had a series of dreams implying that one day his entire family would bow down and worship him. Being young, and perhaps careless, Joseph described these dreams to his father and brothers. The text seems to indicate that his sharing of dreams pushed his brothers over the edge.

Sometime after that, Joseph was sent to Shechem by his father to check on his brothers and the flocks they were tending. Joseph was informed by a stranger that his brothers had moved on to Dothan. Determined to accomplish his mission, he set out to find his brothers in Dothan—about twenty-five miles away. When his brothers saw him coming, they plotted to put him to death. When he arrived, they stripped him and threw him into a pit. Then they sat down to eat dinner.

At this point in the narrative we might expect some divine intervention, If not deliverance, surely some indication that everything was going to work out fine. But nothing happened. God was silent. Joseph sat alone in the bottom of a pit with no guarantee that he would live through the night. No doubt he rehearsed in his mind the events leading up to his imprisonment: his obedience to his father; his willingness to go the extra mile; and now this. It did not make any sense; it was not his fault that his father loved him more than the others. It was not fair. And still, God was seemingly nowhere to be found.

Egypt Bound

As "luck" would have it, a caravan of Ishmaelite traders was passing by. To avoid having the blood of their own kin on their hands, Joseph's brothers sold him to the Ishmaelites. For the next several days, and possibly weeks, Joseph traveled as a slave in the company of the Ishmaelites. Night after night he lay out under the stars wondering, no doubt, why all of this was happening. He knew the stories of his great-grandfather. He had heard how God had spoken to Abraham on several occasions. Certainly he wondered, Why doesn't God speak to me now? But God remained silent.

In Egypt Joseph was sold to Potiphar, the captain of Pharaoh's bodyguard. His master recognized that Joseph was special. Every project Joseph undertook prospered. Eventually Potiphar made him the overseer of the entire house. The Bible tells us that Potiphar did not concern himself with anything except the food he ate (see Gen. 39:6).

Now we might be tempted to think, Well,

that is just like a Bible story; everything worked out fine for Joseph. But what we forget is that Joseph did not show up on Monday and get promoted to overseer on Friday! The best we can tell, Joseph was in Potiphar's service anywhere from five to ten years. And the text seems to imply that Joseph's career as overseer was short-lived. Who knows how long he cleaned out the stables or slopped the pigs? Who knows the type of living quarters he had or who he had to share them with? And regardless of his eventual rank in Potiphar's home, he was still a slave. He was still far away from home. And through all of this, God was silent!

Nothing Lasts Forever

The author of Genesis prepares for the next chapter in Joseph's life when he writes,

> Now Joseph was handsome in form
> and appearance.   —Genesis 39:6

It certainly was not Joseph's fault that he was good-looking. Nor was it his choice to be the overseer of Potiphar's home. But the combination of these two things was more than Potiphar's wife could bear:

His master's wife looked with desire
at Joseph, and she said, "Lie with me!"
—Genesis 39:7

Once again Joseph did the right thing. But the right thing got him into trouble. He refused to get involved with his master's wife. She became angry and accused him of trying to rape her. Just as things were beginning to pick up, Joseph found himself in prison.

Can You Relate?

I hope that by now you are beginning to relate to Joseph. I sure can. There is nothing more bewildering than doing what is right and then watching things fall apart. Or what about adversity that comes as a result of things over which you have no control? Every time I deal with an individual suffering from something that happened during childhood, I think, Lord, it was not this person's decision to be born into that home. Why should this person have to suffer? When I stand at the bedsides of persons suffering from cancer or some other disease, I find myself asking the same question.

You did not pick your parents; yet you

may be dealing with things that stem from their problems. You may have lost a job over something that was not your fault at all. But you are the one who is suffering. Maybe you are one of those women who did your best to respond properly to a husband who was impossible to live with, and now he has abandoned you and your children. Situations such as these make for difficult questions. They seem to justify in our minds the line of thinking that goes like this: If there was a God in heaven, He would not sit idly by while I suffer. Many people have had irreparable damage done to their faith as a result of adversity. That is why this story is such an important one.

One Step Up, Two Steps Back

There is no way of knowing exactly how long Joseph was in prison. We know he was there for more than two years (see Gen. 41:1). It could have been as many as eight or nine. Imagine spending the next few years of your life in a foreign prison. Not awaiting a trial of any kind. Joseph was a slave. He had no rights or avenue of appeal. There was no one to plead his case to Pharaoh. No family to pay a visit. He was sent to prison to rot. And for what reason? Faithfulness to a God who certainly did not seem to be showing much faithfulness in return. Joseph had been outspoken about his faith (see Gen. 39:9). He was doing his best to remain loyal. But he received no blessing in return. Things only got worse. And God was agonizingly silent.

As time passed, Joseph was again recognized as responsible and trustworthy. Eventually, the chief jailer made Joseph the supervisor for the whole jail. Remember, however, we do not know how long he was treated like an ordinary criminal. In two verses the writer of Genesis takes Joseph from being a prisoner to being in charge of the prison. But it is not unrealistic to assume that months and possibly even years passed by before Joseph was recognized as one who could be trusted. And even then, God was silent.

Rather abruptly we are introduced to two new characters, the king's baker and cupbearer. There is no apparent connection between these two and Joseph other than the fact that they are thrown into the same prison. And yet as God would have it, these men play a crucial role in fulfilling His plan.

We are not told why these men were thrown into prison, only that they were. As "fate" would have it, the captain of the bodyguard put these men under Joseph's care. The writer tells us that they were there "for some time." This is another indication that the events described here were separated by long stretches of time, perhaps months or even years. One night, after they had been there a while, each of these men had a dream. When they woke up, the expression on each man's face was such that it was clear to Joseph that something was wrong. Joseph asked,

Why are your faces so sad today?
—Genesis 40:7

They answered,

We have had a dream and there is no one to interpret it.   —Genesis 40:8

Once again, Joseph's unshakable faith in God expresses itself:

Do not interpretations belong to God?
—Genesis 40:8

After all he had been through and with no hope of ever being released from prison, Joseph's faith remained solid, and he was willing to express that faith in God.

Joseph listened carefully as each man described his dream. Then he told them what they meant. The baker was to be executed. The cupbearer, however, would be restored to his previous place of honor. Joseph's response to the cupbearer assures us that Joseph was as human as the rest of us. He said,

> Keep me in mind when it goes well with you, and please do me a kindness by mentioning me to Pharaoh, and get me out of this house. For I was in fact kidnapped from the land of the Hebrews, and even here I have done nothing that they should have put me into the dungeon.
> —Genesis 40:14–15

Joseph may have had faith in God, but he wanted out of prison as badly as any of us would. But once again, it seemed as if God had forgotten Joseph. When the cupbearer was restored, the Scripture tells us,

> Yet the chief cupbearer did not remember Joseph, but forgot him.
> —Genesis 40:23

Do you ever feel as if God has forgotten you? Maybe you have begged God to change your spouse, but you see no change. You may be addicted to some form of narcotic, and it is as if your prayers get no higher than the ceiling. I can't help but believe that every believer has felt forgotten at one point or another, felt as if God is too busy or has His mind on something else.

A Forgotten Family

Dr. W. A. Criswell, pastor of the First Baptist Church of Dallas, tells a story about a family he went to visit years ago when the oil business was booming. This particular family lived in an area where oil companies were buying the oil rights to people's property left and right. Throughout the area families were becoming wealthy overnight as oil was discovered on their property. When Dr. Criswell drove up to this particular family's property, he noticed a peculiar thing, however. There were no oil wells. On the land adjoining their property there were several wells pumping away, but not a single one on the property of the family he had come to visit.

He was greeted at the door by a very dejected looking woman whom he assumed correctly to be the lady of the house. Her husband came in, offered Dr. Criswell a seat, and told his "sad" tale. "Pastor," he said, "God has forgotten us. You see, about a year ago oil was found in this area. Engineers came in and assured everyone in our community that eventually we would be rich beyond our wildest dreams. Well, we saw this as the hand of God. A few weeks later crews came in and began digging around on property all over this area. Wells sprung up everywhere. We knew it was just a matter of time until they would begin digging on our property. But it never happened. Dr. Criswell, God overlooked us. They discovered oil on both sides of our property and even on the property behind us—but not a drop on our land. Our neighbors are selling their homes and moving into the city, and we are left out here alone."

I imagine Joseph must have felt pretty lonely sitting in that Egyptian dungeon. We don't know for sure, but he probably felt betrayed as well. For all he knew, the cupbearer purposely did not tell Pharaoh about him. Once again Joseph suffered as a result of trying to do right. And for two more years he remained a prisoner of Egypt. Two years of wondering why God was letting this happen to him. Two years of battling back and forth in his mind as to whether or not the cupbearer had forgotten about him or just did not care. Two years to rehearse mentally the things that had taken place with his brothers, Potiphar, Potiphar's wife, and now this. Two long years—and God was silent.

Meanwhile . . .

Now it happened at the end of two full years that Pharaoh had a dream, and . . . it came about in the morning that his spirit was troubled, so he sent and called for all the magicians of Egypt, and all its wise men. And Pharaoh told them his dreams, but there was no one who could interpret them to Pharaoh.
                                        —Genesis 41:1–8

It was at this point that the cupbearer finally remembered Joseph. They got him out of the dungeon, shaved him, gave him clean clothes, and brought him before Pharaoh.

And Pharaoh said to Joseph, "I have had a dream, but no one can interpret it; and I have heard it said about you, that when you hear a dream you can interpret it."   —Genesis 41:15

Put yourself in Joseph's place for a minute. How would you have responded to Pharaoh? I know what I would have said: "Before I interpret any dream, we need to make a little deal. First of all, no more prison! Second, where is that sorry cupbearer; I ought to. . . ."

But the words that uttered from Joseph's mouth defy all human explanation. There was no bitterness—though he had good reason to be bitter. He did not speak in anger— though I believe I would have been extremely angry. He did not talk about the wrongs that had been done to him. He simply looked at Pharaoh, the most powerful man in the world at that time, and said,

It is not in me; God will give Pharaoh
a favorable answer.
          —Genesis 41:16

And God did give Pharaoh an answer. Pharaoh was so impressed with Joseph that he made him second in command. In one brief moment Joseph went from a hopeless foreign slave to second in command of the most powerful nation on earth. After thirteen years of misery, something good finally happened.

Silent, but Not Still

What happened, however, was much more fantastic than anything Joseph could have ever hoped for. Joseph did not know that God was setting the stage for a key move in His plan to bring salvation to the world. For God had decided to rear His chosen people, through whom the Messiah would later come, as slaves to a pagan nation. Then by miraculously freeing them from a world-renowned power, He would demonstrate to every nation that He was the only true and living God. Along with that, His people would have a heritage of faith and a picture of what the Messiah would one day do for every nation.

The problem (humanly speaking) was how to get His people out of the land He had given to them through Abraham and to the land of a foreign nation. Second, they had to be welcomed there initially and given enough freedom to live together and multiply. So God chose to accomplish all of that through one man—Joseph. Once he was appointed second in command, there was almost nothing he could not do, including invite his entire family to Egypt to settle during the famine that just "happened" to take place a few years later. As long as he was alive, he could guarantee their safety and freedom. Joseph was the key player in one of the most strategic episodes in the story of salvation, and he never knew it!

If anything is clear from the story of Joseph, it is this: God's silence is in no way indicative of His activity or involvement in our lives. He may be silent, but He is not still. We assume that since we are not hearing anything He must not be doing anything. We judge God's interest and involvement by what we see and hear.

In the same vein, we are guilty of judging God's involvement in our lives by how favorable or unfavorable our circumstances are. As long as things are great, we have no doubt that God is with us—watching over us, protecting us, providing for us. But as soon as adversity comes along, we think, Lord, where are You? Why don't You do something? Are You paying attention?

God's involvement and interest in our lives cannot be judged by the nature of our circumstances. His involvement is measured by two things: first of all, the development of our character, and second, the fulfillment of His plan. Joseph spent about thirteen years facing one adversity after another. And God was involved every step of the way. It was through those adversities that He was accomplishing His will. And God will use adversity to accomplish His will in our lives as well.

In the Meantime . . .

"So what am I supposed to do in the meantime?" you may ask. The answer to that is simple, though it is not necessarily easy. Trust God. That answer may seem too simplistic for your complicated set of circumstances. And in the rest of this book I certainly plan to elaborate. But even if this was the last chapter, consider your options. If you are not going to trust God, what are you going to do? To take things in your own hands is to run the most certain risk of leaping out of the frying pan into the fire. Ask Jonah! Actually, you probably do not even have to think any further than your own experience. When have you ever turned your back on God's plan and come out a winner?

You say, "But you don't understand my circumstances." And you may be right. But think about Joseph. No friends, no family, no church, no freedom, no money, no Bible, no apparent answers from God. Yet he remained faithful—and so did his heavenly Father.

When God is silent, you have only one reasonable option—trust Him; hang in there; wait on Him. He may be quiet, but He has not quit on you.

Back at the Ranch

Now I want to tell you what finally happened to the family who had no oil on their land. A few years later Dr. Criswell ran into the father of that family. He was smiling from ear to ear. Dr. Criswell assumed they had finally found oil on his property. "Quite the contrary," the man replied. "They never found any oil, and I am glad of it." This certainly took the pastor by surprise. "The strangest thing happened," he continued. "All our neighbors moved to the city and bought big expensive houses and new cars. They sent their kids to the finest schools. Most of them joined country clubs. But before too long that lifestyle began to take its toll. One by one their marriages started breaking up. Their kids rebelled. We don't know of any that are still attending church on a regular basis. Pastor, God did us a big favor by not putting any oil on our land. We are all still together and love each other like never before. We thank Him every day for giving us what is important and protecting us from the things that aren't."

God had not forgotten that family. But it took them a while to understand. My friend, God has not forgotten you. He may be silent, but He is not still. Remember, God's silence is always amplified by the anguish of adversity. But through even the gravest adversity, He is working to develop your character and accomplish His will for your life.

4

Justice for All

If God is all-powerful, He certainly has the ability to put an end to injustice. If He is a righteous and just God, He surely must desire to do so. Yet we live in a world full of injustice. What's up?

This question comes in many forms, usually not quite this cut-and-dried. It is the question behind an abandoned wife's tears of sorrow. It is the reason for the doubtful look of a child who has been molested. It is the cause of uncertainty for the man who is fired over some trivial matter only months before retirement. "If God is just, why does He allow injustice to touch the lives of those He loves?"

All of us have asked this question at one

time or another. If not on our own behalf, on behalf of a friend or relative. But we are not the first to be slapped in the face with the cold, hard realities of injustice in this world. In the first century the nation of Israel was saturated with injustice of every kind. Having been taken over by the Roman Empire, they were at the mercy of a foreign power. The Romans taxed the Jews heavily in order to pay for their military campaigns in other parts of the world. They confiscated the best land. They took the best produce. They set up their own government and appointed their own governors and magistrates.

At a time when the people desperately needed guidance from their religious leaders, there was none to be found. They had sold out to the Romans. In exchange for places of honor and privilege, the Pharisees had promised to encourage the Jews to work with Rome, not against her. The religious leaders became pawns the Romans used to keep peace.

Into this oppressive atmosphere of injustice befouled by long-standing frustrations walked the Lord Jesus. As news of His ministry spread, so did rumors that this, in fact, might be the Messiah. Expectations began to rise, for the people expected the Messiah to bring about social, political, and religious reform when He came. They were looking to the Messiah to reestablish justice in the land. And so Jesus went about His Father's business knowing that the pressure was on to bring about major reform. The expectations and desires of the people in Jesus' day were much like our own. They wanted justice. They were tired of suffering unjustly. They were ready for God to do something.

In response to the frustration and hopelessness He sensed among the people, Jesus told the following parable:

> There was in a certain city a judge who did not fear God, and did not respect man. And there was a widow in that city, and she kept coming to him, saying, "Give me legal protection from my opponent." And for a while he was unwilling; but afterward he said to himself, "Even though I do not fear God nor respect man, yet because this widow bothers me, I will give her legal protection, lest by continually coming she wear me out." And the Lord said, "Hear what the unrighteous judge said; now shall not God bring about justice for His elect, who cry to

Him day and night, and will He delay long over them? I tell you that He will bring about justice for them speedily. However, when the Son of Man comes, will He find faith on the earth?"   —Luke 18:2–8

Jesus presents a worst case scenario of a judge who cares about no one and a widow who has very few, if any, rights. She needs justice. And apparently this unrighteous judge is her only hope. Day after day she goes to him begging for help and finds none. Finally this judge thinks to himself, If I don't do something, this woman is going to drive me crazy. Not only that, she could ruin my reputation. So he gives in and helps her out.

A cursory reading would seem to indicate that the point of the parable is this: if you bother God long enough, He will grant you justice. But that is not Christ's point at all. The parable is presented in such a way as to set up a comparison between an unrighteous judge and a righteous God. The point Jesus is making is this: if an unrighteous judge can be convinced to bring about justice for a widow with whom he has no relationship or invested interest, how much more confident should we be that a righteous God will bring about justice for His elect. In case His listeners are unclear about the point He is making, Jesus comes right out and says, "I tell you that He [God] will bring about justice for them speedily."

The bottom line is that God will bring about justice for the elect, the elect being those who have expressed faith in Christ. I imagine this brought some sense of comfort to His audience as it does to those of us who have wondered from time to time whether or not there would ever be justice on the earth. But I also imagine they had the same burning question you and I are left asking. When? When is God going to bring about justice for the elect? When are the unjust going to be punished? When are those who have been treated unfairly going to be avenged?

A Scheduling Problem

Jesus knew His words would raise questions concerning the timing of this promised justice. He knows us so well that He anticipated our response to His answer. So He presents His answer in the form of a question, thereby putting the ball back into our court before we have time to argue. He says,

"When the Son of Man comes, will He find faith on the earth?"

There will be justice for the elect when Christ returns the second time. No doubt there were looks of confusion and dismay on the faces of those to whom He spoke that day. They must have thought, When the Son of Man comes? He is already here! For us, His response does not bring so much confusion as it does disappointment because we do not want to wait until Christ comes again to see justice prevail. We want it now!

It is no wonder. In the past twenty or so years increasing emphasis has been placed on what God will do for us now. Look at the book titles in your local Christian bookstore; listen to the sermons that fill the airwaves every Sunday morning. "Believe today and be healed tomorrow. Give today and God will bless you tomorrow." In our quest to see God do something in our lives we have lost sight of the big picture. We have forgotten what God is doing in the realm of world history. We have overlooked the fact that we live in a sinful, wicked age under a curse from God. Even nature groans waiting to be set free (see Rom. 8:18–25).

The ultimate answer to the problem of suffering and injustice in the world is the return of the Lord Jesus Christ. At His return all men and women must stand and give an account for what they have done. In the book of Revelation the apostle John describes it this way:

> And I saw a great white throne and Him who sat upon it, from whose presence earth and heaven fled away, and no place was found for them. And I saw the dead, the great and the small, standing before the throne, and books were opened; and another book was opened, which is the book of life; and the dead were judged from the things which were written in the books, according to their deeds. . . . and they were judged, every one of them according to their deeds.
> —Revelation 20:11–13

John makes it clear that those who stand at the great white throne of judgment will be judged according to their deeds. The apostle Paul echoed the same idea when he wrote,

> For we must all appear before the judgment seat of Christ, that each one

may be recompensed for his deeds in the body, according to what he has done, whether good or bad.
— 2 Corinthians 5:10

This passage is especially interesting for two reasons. First, believers are included in this judgment. Second, the term "recompensed" means "paid back." We will be paid back for our deeds, whether they are good or bad. That means every crooked salesman, every dishonest employee or employer, every unfaithful husband, and on and on we could go. On that day justice will come to God's elect. They will be avenged!

But There's More!

But that is only half the story. Not only will the unjust be dealt with according to what they have done, the righteous will be rewarded. In the Sermon on the Mount Jesus said that those who suffer unjust treatment will have a "great" reward in heaven (see Matt. 5:10). The elect who have been abused, abandoned, stolen from, taken advantage of—all will be rewarded for their pain.

For this finds **favor**, if for the sake of conscience toward God a man bears up under sorrows when suffering unjustly. . . . when you do what is right and suffer for it you patiently endure it, this finds **favor** with God. For you have been called for this purpose, since Christ also suffered for you, leaving you an example for you to follow in His steps.
—1 Peter 2:19–21 (emphasis mine)

Peter says that when we are treated unjustly God looks down from heaven and smiles; He finds "favor" in it. God gets excited when we suffer unjustly. Why? Because that is what we have been called to do. We should not be surprised when we are treated unjustly. In fact, we should be surprised when we are not! Just as Christ suffered unjust treatment, so must we.

To sum up, let all be harmonious, sympathetic, brotherly, kindhearted, and humble in spirit; not returning evil for evil, or insult for insult, but giving a blessing instead; for you were called for the very purpose that

you might inherit a blessing.
—1 Peter 3:8–9

Those who suffer unjustly will not only have their cause avenged by God, they will inherit a blessing as well. James refers to this blessing as the "crown of life" (see James 1:12). No one knows exactly what this will be. But the context of these verses seems to indicate that whatever it is it will more than make up for the injustice we have suffered.

First Things First

Think about something for a minute. We want justice now. We don't want to wait for the Lord's return. But did you know that not even the murder of the Son of God has been avenged? The most hideous crime in the history of mankind has yet to come to trial. Somewhere there sits the group of men responsible for the murder of Christ. Though the crime took place many years ago, their case has not yet been tried. God has chosen to wait for Christ's return to judge those who crucified His Son. My friend, if God has chosen to delay justice for that case, who are we to demand that our case take precedent?

God knows when we suffer unjustly. Not

only does He know about it, He is taking notes, for the Scriptures promise that we will be judged according to our works. That being the case, then someone, somewhere, must be taking all of this down! God has not abandoned you to the whims and wishes of those who are more powerful. He knows when His children are overlooked for advancement because of their religious views. Young lady, He knows when less talented women are advanced past you because you refuse to compromise morally. He sees the abandoned mother who never knows from month to month if her estranged husband is going to send a check. God is taking it all in. He has already appointed a prosecuting attorney, a jury, and a judge. And they are all the same person—the Lord Jesus. On that court date He will bring about justice for His elect.

Until Then . . .

So what are we to do in the meantime? At this juncture Jesus' question takes on a great deal of meaning.

> However, when the Son of Man comes, will He find faith on the earth?
> —Luke 18:8

Jesus was asking whether or not any of the elect would remain faithful while justice was delayed. Would He return to find that the elect had taken matters into their own hands? Would He return to find that they had given up hope and abandoned the faith altogether? The very fact that Jesus would ask such a question lets us know how in tune with us He really is. He knows how difficult it is for us to wait. He is aware of the sinking feeling we have felt at some point when we realize we have been taken advantage of or used.

In asking this question, Jesus gives us our assignment: remain faithful; pray for justice; look expectantly for the judge. By faithfulness, He means simply doing all we know to do while trusting Him with everything else. For some, that means picking up the pieces of a shattered marriage and rebuilding from the inside out. For others, it means starting a new career.

If we look beyond the details of our external world, faithfulness can go much deeper. For some, it means repenting of doubt and anger toward God. Perhaps somewhere in your past you were dealt a devastating blow emotionally or even physically. At that point you could not reconcile the conflict of such injustice with the existence of a loving God. And you walked away from the Lord.

My friend, He understands. It is no coincidence that you are reading these lines. Even now God is trying to bring you back to Himself. Faithfulness for you may mean reestablishing your faith in God, confessing your doubt, and learning all over again to walk by faith.

Let It Go

For some, faithfulness will mean releasing years of bitterness and vengeance that have been stored up on the inside. Perhaps you lie in bed at night and have imaginary conversations with your ex-wife. Or you daydream about getting back at your boss. Or you scheme up ways to embarrass those who have treated you unjustly. Do you realize that by allowing such things to continue, you are in effect saying to God, "I don't trust You to bring about justice in this matter. You need my help"? God does not need your help. He has appointed Christ to judge the wicked and defend the innocent. If you store up hatred and animosity toward those who have hurt you, the injury is only deepened. Those around you will suffer, for bitterness is like poison. It harms everything it touches.

There is no use in allowing persons who have harmed you to harm you further. Release all that anger to the Lord. Tell Him right now that you recognize Him as your judge and your avenger. Ask Him to show you how to put the pieces of your life back together. It won't happen overnight. But He is faithful. And all He requires of you is that you remain faithful as well, knowing that He will bring about justice for His elect!

> When the Son of Man returns to claim
>   His own,
> He is faithful.
> When the Judge of all mankind takes His
>   throne,
> He is true.
> And when I stand without excuse there in
>   His presence,
> Judged for what I did and did not do,
> Find me faithful,
> Find me true!

5

Advancing Through Adversity

Biblical narratives such as those of Lazarus and Joseph make one point undeniably clear: God uses adversity in the lives of His children. Adversity, however, is not simply a tool. It is God's most effective tool for the advancement of our spiritual lives. The circumstances and events that we see as setbacks are oftentimes the very things that launch us into periods of intense spiritual growth. Once we begin to understand this, and accept it as a spiritual fact of life, adversity becomes easier to bear.

It is within the context of this principle that Paul was able to say,

> All things work together for good to those who love God, to those who are called according to His purpose.
>
> —Romans 8:28, NKJV

This is a conditional promise. For the person who does not love God and thus is not interested in knowing Him or growing spiritually, all things do not necessarily work for good because sometimes that "good" is the lesson or depth of character developed as a result of adversity. From God's perspective, it is good if we learn to be patient. It is good if we learn to love those who are unattractive. God values character far more than wealth, prominence, health, or many of the other things we hold dear.

Whose Good?

The "good" of Romans 8:28 is not necessarily the story of a man who loses his job and in the end gets a better one. It may be the story of a man who loses his job and comes to a greater understanding of what it means to trust God daily. The "good" of Romans 8:28 is not necessarily the story of a young woman who loses her love only to

. . . there is
nothing worse
than a life
filled with
adversity from
which nothing
good ever
comes.

find a better catch later on. Instead it could be the story of a woman who through the tragedy of a lost love discovers God's call to enter full-time Christian service.

The reason so many of us struggle so intensely with adversity is that we have yet to adopt God's perspective and priorities. As you read the lives of biblical characters, you will notice quickly that their stories do not end with, "And they lived happily ever after." Oftentimes, their stories seem to end just the opposite way. Moses died in the desert just a few miles from the Promised Land. Paul, according to tradition, was beheaded by Nero. Many of the disciples were martyred.

Are we to conclude from these examples that God has no interest in His children being happy? No! We are told that heaven will be a place of great rejoicing and happiness. But God wants far more for us than simply living a life that is problem-free. The fact is, the people who have no problems as we usually think of them are some of the most unhappy people in the world. They are usually bored. After a while, their boredom drives them to things that cause them problems. It is a mistake to think that a problem-free life is a happy life.

Happiness Defined

"Happiness," the way God defines it, "is a state of well-being that reaches deep into the soul of a man or woman." Its context is much broader than mere circumstance. Its effect on the emotions goes beyond momentary excitement. And the means by which one comes about it is not by the acquisition of more things. Neither is it the rearrangement of circumstances. The happiness God desires for His children comes only through the process of spiritual growth and maturity. Apart from that, there is no lasting happiness.

God does want us to be happy, but not the happiness advocated by the world. His desire for our happiness is expressed by His desire for us to "grow up" spiritually. The apostle Paul put it this way:

> As a result, we are no longer to be children, tossed here and there by waves, and carried about by every wind of doctrine, by the trickery of men, by craftiness in deceitful scheming; but speaking the truth in love, **we are to grow up** in all aspects into Him, who is the head, even Christ.
> —Ephesians 4:14–15 (emphasis mine)

To remain spiritually immature is to run the risk of eventually abandoning the faith. To adopt a worldview or life philosophy other than God's is to embrace a lie. No one has ever been "happy" for very long embracing a lie. Therefore, spiritual growth is imperative from God's point of view not only for our spiritual well-being, but for our general happiness as well. Continual spiritual growth, then, is the means by which God keeps us in tune with His purposes for our lives.

Since adversity is God's most effective tool insofar as spiritual growth is concerned, the degree to which we desire to grow spiritually corresponds to our ability to handle adversity successfully. Men or women who are only marginally interested in maturing as Christians will have a difficult time with adversity. Their tendency will be to blame God and become bitter. Instead of seeing adversity as something God is trying to do for them, they will see it as something He is doing to them. It is all a matter of priority and perspective. If our priorities are ease, comfort, and pleasure, we will have little tolerance for adversity. We will see it as an interruption rather than a part of God's plan for us.

But when we allow God to shape our priorities, adversity takes on a whole new meaning. We see it as an integral part of what God is doing in our lives. We begin to understand that adversity is sometimes a means to greater joy and peace. We don't panic and assume God has forgotten about us. Rather we can rejoice. Why? Because God is in the process of bringing about another good in our life.

Spiritual men and women emerge from adversity excited about what God has taught them. Carnal men and women often emerge bitter and angry with God for what He "put them through." They are quick to point out that "all things don't work together for good," conveniently ignoring the second half of the verse.

An Annual Lesson

It seems that I have to learn this same lesson at least once every year. I am an achievement-oriented person; I like to see projects begun and completed. I like to have several projects going at the same time. I enjoy setting goals. I am always writing out to-do lists. Because of my go-go-go personality and lifestyle, nothing is more frustrating to me than getting sick. What a waste of time! First, I become angry. "Lord, do You know what all I have going on? I don't have time to be sick." Then, I remember I am in the ministry and try to sound spiritual. "Lord, Your work is suffering! If I don't get well quick, what is going to happen to the ministry?"

I finally realize that God is not impressed with my commitment to His work and that He cannot be bribed or manipulated. Only then do I begin to ask the right questions: "Lord, what are You saying to me? What do You want me to learn? What about my lifestyle needs to be changed or eliminated?" For some reason, it is not until I am flat on my back that I am willing to take the time to ask these kinds of questions. The rest of the time I am too busy doing the "work of the Lord."

During these times, God has taught me some of the most exciting things I have ever learned. When I return to the pulpit, I am full of insight and enthusiasm. This has happened so many times now that my congregation gets excited when I get sick. Not because they want me to be sick, but because of the blessing they receive when I am back on my feet and able to share what the Lord has taught me.

That's Easy for You to Say

I realize that the adversity you are facing in your life may be of a far more serious nature than my annual bout with the flu or some other seasonal ailment. And I am painfully aware of the tendency in literature and sermons to oversimplify when it comes to the subject of adversity. But the truth is, God wants to use the adversity you are facing right now to advance your spiritual growth. The Bible gives us plenty of reason to believe that God could erase all adversity from our lives with just a word. But experience tells us He has chosen not to do that. Far more important than our ease, comfort, and pleasure is our spiritual growth.

If we are believers—that is, we have put our trust in Christ's death on the cross to be the payment for our sin—God has us in school. He is in the process of teaching us about Himself: His faithfulness, His goodness, His compassion, and His holiness. Just like any other school, some classes are more appealing than others. And if we are honest, Adversity 101 is not one of our favorite classes. But it is essential if we are to "grow up" in the Lord.

The Old Standby

The most-quoted verse in all the Bible when it comes to the topic of adversity is James 1:2. Unfortunately, verses like this one become so familiar that they lose their punch after a while. That being the case, I purposely waited until this chapter to bring it up.

As much as we may hate to admit it, the truth of James's words is foundational. It serves as the basis upon which our understanding of adversity rests. He writes,

> Consider it all joy, my brethren, when you encounter various trials, knowing that the testing of your faith produces endurance. And let endurance have its perfect result, that you may be perfect and complete, lacking in nothing.
> —James 1:2–4

We need to take note of several things in these verses. First of all, our initial response to trials is to be joy. Upon first glance James seems to be demonstrating an incredible amount of insensitivity. When I am facing a crisis in my life, the last thing I want is some preacher telling me to rejoice! However, James is not telling us to be joyous because of the trial. There is nothing joyous about trials in and of themselves. We are only deceiving ourselves when we dutifully and unenthusiastically say, "Praise the Lord," every time something goes wrong.

James is very clear as to why we are to be joyous in the midst of adversity. He states it, however, in the form of an assumption rather than a reason. James assumes that his readers are so committed to spiritual growth that when they understand that trials lead to more spiritual growth, they will rejoice because of the end result—growth! The "testing" of our faith produces "endurance." Endurance is a maturing factor. The term "perfect" carries with it the idea of maturity. Whenever persons are forced to endure hardship, they mature in some fashion. James says that endurance can bring about a great deal of maturity in individuals.

James warns that there is a way to interrupt this maturing process. He instructs his readers to "let endurance have its perfect result." The implication is that by reacting to adversity incorrectly, we short-circuit the maturing process. By resisting adversity, we rob ourselves of the work God desires to do in our lives. We put off the very thing God sent the adversity into our lives to accomplish.

I know of several people who are mad at God because of the adversity that has come their way. One particular fellow refuses to step foot inside the church because he did not get the promotion he thought he deserved. Another lady is mad because God did not stop her daughter from marrying an unbeliever. The tragedy in each case is that these people have put themselves on the sidelines spiritually. They cannot advance one more inch spiritually until they change their perspective on adversity. The very thing God allowed into their lives as an incentive to grow has put them into a spiritual coma. Why? Because they refused to "let endurance have its perfect [maturing] result."

Until we are committed to the process of spiritual maturity and growth, we will never be able to take James seriously. There will never be any joy in suffering. James assumed that when the majority of his readers learned that these tests of faith would produce endurance, they would be glowing with excitement.

Rejoice?

You may be thinking, That is ridiculous. How could anyone be so enthusiastic about growing spiritually as to rejoice when confronted with adversity? If that is your attitude, the next few verses of this passage are for you.

> But if any of you lacks wisdom, let him ask of God, who gives to all men generously and without reproach, and it will be given to him. But let him ask in faith without any doubting, for the one who doubts is like the surf of the sea driven and tossed by the wind. For let not that man expect that he will receive anything from the Lord, being a double-minded man, unstable in all his ways.   —James 1:5–8

James was not out of touch with the real world. He realized how strange it sounded to tell people to rejoice in the midst of trials. So he followed up by saying, "Hey, if you find that hard to accept, ask the Lord to make it clear to you." That is what he means by asking for wisdom. Wisdom is the ability to see things from God's perspective; it is usually a matter of getting the big picture. The big picture in this case is God's ultimate desire for His children—spiritual maturity.

For a long time I had trouble accepting this connection between adversity and growth. I could grasp the connection mentally, but emotionally it was difficult to take. I thought all this talk about God's using illness and tragedy and other forms of adversity to teach people things was just a way to cover for Him. People like to be able to explain things away, and I assumed this was just another means of dealing with what could not otherwise be explained.

My problem, when I got right down to it, was faith. It was hard for me to accept that God is so intent on bringing us to maturity that He is willing to let us suffer. In His economy, adversity is a small price to pay for the benefits of spiritual growth. As I studied passages such as the ones we have already examined, it became clear to me that the issue was not whether or not I thought adversity was a fair trade-off for spiritual growth. The issue was whether or not I was going to take God at His word and begin viewing adversity from that perspective.

I think my wavering back and forth is exactly what James was talking about when he said we must ask "in faith." That is, when God reveals the answer, we must accept it—not debate it, not simply consider it. We are to take God at His word and live by it. Until we are willing to do that, things will never be clear.

Strangely enough, it was not the adversity I was facing in my life that made this principle so difficult to accept. I could readily see the spiritual benefit that came through the adversity in my life. I was disturbed by the things I saw confronting other people: divorces, serious illnesses, the loss of friends, family, and possessions. I would look at their circumstances and think, Lord, are You paying attention? These people did not deserve this! What are You doing?

Over and over again, however, I would go to these people to comfort them and find that God was ministering to them in such a powerful way that they became encouragements to me. Women whose husbands had walked off and left them were praising God for His mercy and provision. I talked to men who lost their jobs but in doing so rediscovered their families and praised God for what happened. I'll never forget a couple who had just lost everything they owned in a fire. After the initial shock wore off, they began to understand why God had allowed it to happen. Before long, they were giving testimony to God's faithfulness and rejoicing that they were able to better understand what really mattered and what does not.

One day I was in a restaurant and noticed that the hostess was wearing a cross. I asked her if she was a Christian. Big tears welled up in her eyes. "You better believe it," she said. As we talked, she told me one of the saddest stories I have ever heard. It was just four days before Christmas, and her husband had walked out on her for another woman. To make matters worse, her daughter and son had turned on her and were planning to spend Christmas with her husband and his girl-friend, leaving this woman with no one to share her holiday. But what issued forth from her lips were not words of criticism and re-sentment. Instead, she was praising God for His sustaining power. She went on to tell about the people to whom she had been able to witness. I sat there amazed.

Stories like these, along with the clear teaching of God's Word, finally convinced me that God could be trusted in the midst of adversity, that He really could work all things together for good if we would adopt His definition of good and accept His sys-tem of priorities. I realized that God knows exactly how much pressure each of us needs to advance in the spiritual life. It was hard for me to stand back and watch others suffer because I was not aware of all God was doing for them on the inside. My perspective was limited to what was taking place on the outside.

Taking the Long Look

Dealing with adversity is like preparing for surgery. By putting our faith in what the doctor has said, we believe we will be better off if we have the surgery. But that does not make it any less painful. By submitting to the hand of a surgeon, we are saying that our ultimate goal is health, even at the cost of pain. Adversity is the same way. It is a means to an end. It is God's tool for the advancement of our spiritual lives.

Perhaps you cannot bring yourself to adopt this attitude. In light of the adversity you or a loved one has faced, it may seem too much like a sugar pill, an excuse Christians use to keep God from looking bad. If that is where you are in your thinking, I want you to contemplate this question: If adversity is not a tool in the hand of God, what is it? What are your options?

You could adopt the philosophy of some who say God is fighting a cosmic battle with evil. In that way of thinking, adversity surfaces when God loses a round. Embracing that form of religion, however, means abandoning Christianity. There is no way the God of the Bible can be made to fit into that worldview. The two are mutually exclusive.

A person could argue that God does not care; therefore, He is unconcerned about the adversity we face. The problem there is that the question of God's love and concern was settled two thousand years ago when God sacrificed what was most precious to Him for the sake of man. The Cross puts to rest any question of love.

One may argue that there is no God. But simply because God does not behave the way we might expect Him to certainly does not disprove His existence. That would be like my determining the existence of my wife based upon how I think a wife should act.

This whole problem of injustice in the world kept C. S. Lewis from embracing Christianity. He assumed, like many, that there could not possibly be a good God in light of all the evil in the world. In *Mere Christianity* he describes his pilgrimage as he tried to cope with this perplexing question.

My argument against God was that the universe seemed so cruel and unjust. But how had I got this idea of just and unjust? A man does not call a line crooked unless he has some idea of a straight line. What was I comparing this universe with when I called it unjust? If the whole show was bad and senseless from A to Z, so to speak, why did I who was supposed to be a part of the show, find myself in such violent reaction against it? . . . Of course I could have given up my idea of justice by saying it was nothing but a private idea of my own. But if I did that, then my argument against God collapsed too—for the argument depended on saying that the world was really unjust, not simply that it did not happen to please my private fancies.

To deny the existence of God based on the presence of adversity and pain is to say that in order to validate His existence God must conduct Himself according to my wishes. Clearly, there are multiple problems with that approach.

There really are no good alternatives when it comes to the question of adversity. Adversity is God's tool to promote growth among His children. To resist this principle is to resist all God wants to do in your life; it is to say no to spiritual growth.

The Crown of Life

James ends this section with an interesting promise:

> Blessed is a man who perseveres under trial; for once he has been approved, he will receive the crown of life, which the Lord has promised to those who love Him.   —James 1:12

Not only does adversity lead to spiritual maturity in this life, it purchases for us a crown of life in the next. God understands the trauma of dealing with adversity. He has not overlooked the sacrifices we are forced to make when adversity comes our way. Therefore, He has provided a special reward for those who "persevere under trial." Once again we are faced with a conditional promise. This reward is reserved for those who willingly accepted the Christ in their lives. These are the ones who understood that God was up to something, that the adversity they faced was the means by which something good would come about in their lives.

Are you persevering? Are you enduring? Or are you resisting? Are you mad at God for what He is doing? My friend, God wants to advance you through the use of adversity. He wants to grow you up and mature you to the point that your character is a mirror image of Christ's. That is His goal for you. And adversity is the means by which He will accomplish it. Why not trust Him? It is futile to resist. Your sorrow will only be magnified, for there is nothing worse than a life filled with adversity from which nothing good ever comes.

Why not tell the Lord, "Lord, I don't like it, but by faith I rejoice that You are up to something good in my life"? Eventually you will begin to see the "good." You will begin to experience peace. You will begin to advance through your adversity.

6

Your Attention, Please!

An old story tells of a farmer who had a mule for sale. He claimed that this mule would obey any command it was given. One prospective customer was somewhat leery of this claim and decided to put the farmer and his mule to the test. So he said to the mule, "Sit down." But the mule just stood there. "Sit," the customer yelled. But nothing happened. He turned to the farmer and said, "You claim this mule will do anything it is told, but I can't get the mule to sit down." The farmer just smiled. He reached down and picked up a two-by-four, then walked over and hit the mule in the head. "Sit," he said.

And the mule sat right down. Turning to the shocked customer, he said, "First, you have to get his attention."

I am afraid that some of us are like that old mule. One of the reasons God allows adversity into our lives is to get our attention. It is easy to get so caught up in our own activities and busy schedules that we lose sight of God. When we focus on our goals, careers, families, and other personal concerns, we neglect to give God the proper priority in our lives. The result is that we lose our spiritual sensitivity.

This process of becoming spiritually insensitive is not something we are usually aware of. It slips up on us slowly. For me, it is usually a matter of overscheduling and allowing myself to get too busy. Whatever the case, God is acutely aware of when we have become too preoccupied with ourselves and our interests. He knows when it is time to plan an interruption to get our attention.

Is There No Other Way?

The question immediately arises: Isn't there some other way of getting our attention? Does it have to be something painful or tragic? Theoretically, the answer is no.

There are certainly other means of gaining one's attention than through adversity. But think about it for a moment. How many sermons have you sat through, keenly aware that what the preacher was talking about applied to you, and then walked right out and did nothing about it? How many times have you heard a testimony that stirred your spirit and sparked a desire in you to live by a higher standard? But again, you were barely out the sanctuary door before some earthly concern flooded your mind and washed away all your noble plans and intentions.

Oftentimes it takes more than a sermon to get our attention. Not even heartfelt conviction is enough. Usually it takes a jolt of some kind to bring us around. C. S. Lewis, in his wonderful little book, *The Problem of Pain*, put it this way:

> God whispers to us in our pleasures,
> speaks in our conscience, but shouts
> in our pains: it is His megaphone to
> rouse a deaf world.

When things are going our way, it is sometimes difficult to turn our thoughts to God. Oh, we all know we should. But it becomes an effort. When all is well, we quickly drift into a state of self-reliance and smugness. Our prayers become lifeless. The Word of God begins to sound unappealing to complacent ears. And to make matters worse, we begin to confuse our sense of well-being with spirituality. When nothing is wrong, we falsely assume that everything is right.

Anyone who has done much in the way of evangelism knows what I am talking about. It is next to impossible for an unbeliever who has no pressing problems to see the need for a Savior. When everything is going fine, why mess it up with God? Why think about death? For that matter, why even worry about tomorrow?

But come back to that same man or woman following an experience of adversity and you will find a completely different attitude. What was of little concern has become the only concern. What at one time was of great importance holds no attraction at all. Suddenly, God has the individual's attention.

Recently my son, Andy, was invited to a Cocaine Anonymous (CA) meeting to present a one-year chip to a friend of his who had been fighting drug addiction for many years. His comment afterward got my attention. He said, "There aren't any atheists in CA." One of the foundational principles upon which

Alcoholics Anonymous (AA), Narcotics Anonymous (NA), and CA are based is that addicts need the help of a higher power if they are to be drug- or alcohol-free. The groups allow members to discover or define for themselves what or who that higher power is. Several confessed that they had little or no time for God before facing up to their addiction. Once they did, however, God, or "the higher power," took on a significant role in their daily lives. All of them recognized their need for help.

Such is the power of adversity. It brings even the strongest and most stubborn of us to our knees. It causes us to loosen our grip on those things that are of little value and cling tightly to the One we know can deliver us.

Blinded by the Light

One of the best illustrations of this principle is what happened to the apostle Paul. He was totally committed to doing what he believed was right—stamping out the existence of the church. He had heard the truth of Jesus preached on several occasions. No doubt he had seen the signs performed by the followers of Christ. But that did not get his attention. He had witnessed the stoning of Stephen. He stood there and watched as Stephen prayed for those who were casting the stones. It is likely that he was one of those who noticed the angelic aura of Stephen's face (see Acts 6:15). But not even that was enough to get Paul's attention.

In the ninth chapter of Acts, Luke records the incident that finally got the attention of the apostle Paul, who was at that time still called Saul of Tarsus. He was on his way to Damascus to seek out and arrest any men or women who were followers of Christ— or "the Way" as it was referred to then. This was not a task he took lightly. Luke informs us that Saul was "breathing threats and murder against the disciples of the Lord" (Acts 9:1). Saul was so given to his task that he is described as one whose every breath was a threat of destruction. He was consumed by his goal.

On his way to Damascus, however, God got his attention. Luke records it this way:

> And it came about that as he journeyed, he was approaching Damascus, and suddenly a light from heaven flashed around him; and he fell to the ground, and heard a voice saying to

him, "Saul, Saul, why are you persecuting Me?" And he said, "Who art
Thou, Lord?" And He said, "I am
Jesus whom you are persecuting, but
rise, and enter the city, and it shall be
told you what you must do." . . . And
Saul got up from the ground, and
though his eyes were open, he could
see nothing; and leading him by the
hand, they brought him into Damascus.

—Acts 9:3–6, 8

In one unforeseen moment, God gained
Saul's undivided attention by striking him
down with a blinding light, humiliating him
in front of all his traveling companions.
Imagine the thoughts that flashed across his
mind as the reality of his condition became
apparent. Blind! Envision this man of prominence and prestige down in the dirt as he
felt his eyes to make sure they were actually open. No doubt Saul thought he was
permanently blind. And that thought must
have paralyzed him with fear.

God had Saul exactly where He wanted
him. And Saul was more than ready to listen. "Why are you persecuting Me?" the Lord
asked. Saul had not thought about what he

was doing from that perspective. He never imagined that he was persecuting Jesus; Jesus was dead! Or was He? As the truth settled in, Saul realized his error. And a few days later he was proclaiming Jesus in the synagogues (see Acts 9:20).

When we read or hear a story such as that one, it is easy to see the value of adversity. If indeed it took temporary blindness and humiliation to get Paul's attention, it was certainly worth it, for through him the gospel was preached and churches were planted across the Roman world of his day. Paul was the first to take the Great Commission seriously. He was one of the first to realize that the gospel was to be preached to Gentiles as well as Jews. When we think about all he accomplished, we can understand how God could have justified almost anything to get his attention.

A Look into the Future

But what about you? What could God accomplish through you if He had your undivided attention and loyalty? We forget sometimes that when God looks at our lives, He sees not only our past, but our potential for the future as well. He knows what He could accomplish through our gifts and talents if we were completely His. He is aware of the people watching our lives, judging the merits of Christianity by the consistency of our lifestyle. He sees that lost soul with whom we will have an opportunity to share—if we are spiritually on track at the time of our encounter. He knows who among us could be great preachers or writers or debaters or teachers. He is aware of what could happen through us if we were available for His purposes. And from the perspective of eternity, whatever it would take to get our attention would be worth it.

I Remembered the Lord

The most obvious illustration of this principle in the Scriptures is the story of Jonah. Whereas Paul was ignorant of the truth, Jonah knew the truth all too well, but decided to run from it. Chances are, most of us will probably identify with Jonah more easily than we can with Paul. Rarely are we ignorant of what God wants from us. We are not suffering from a lack of information. What we lack is the willingness to obey. When God uses adversity to get my attention, it is rarely for the purpose of telling me something new.

Usually, He is reminding me of something I either have forgotten or have purposely chosen to ignore.

In the case of Jonah, God used adversity to refocus his attention on what he had originally been asked to do. As Jonah sloshed about in the belly of the fish—fighting for his life—he remembered! Jonah said,

> While I was fainting away,
> I remembered the LORD;
> And my prayer came to Thee.
>   —Jonah 2:7

I bet it did! He went on,

> Those who regard vain idols
> Forsake their faithfulness,
> But I will sacrifice to Thee
> With the voice of thanksgiving.
> That which I have vowed I will pay.
>   —Jonah 2:8–9

To put it mildly, Jonah rededicated his life to the Lord. Why? Because he felt compassion for the lost people in Nineveh? No. In fact he was sorry when they repented. Jonah decided to obey God because in the belly of that fish he got a good dose of reality. Simply put, God is in charge! That is reason enough to obey.

This week I received a letter from an old friend. His story is one I have heard many times in the course of my ministry. At seventeen he felt called to preach. He resisted that call. He fought it through college and graduate school. His struggle finally turned him away from the Lord altogether. It was while he was outside the will of God that he chose both his wife and his career. In time he lost both. Now, almost twenty-five years later, he is ready to serve the Lord. I believe God will use this man—as He has so many others with similar stories. But it was only after He had taken everything this man valued that He finally had my friend's attention.

To some, this whole notion may sound cruel and unfair. And to be honest, in the midst of situations where God was working to gain my undivided attention, I had my doubts as well. But we are the ones who are unfair if for one moment we assign to God the label of cruel. Our stubbornness and insensitivity to His Spirit cause Him to resort to those things we find unpleasant. Our preoccupation and infatuation with the things of this world diminish our spiritual sensitivity. If we are really honest, we leave God no choice.

If you are facing adversity in your life, God may be trying to get your attention. He may be trying to draw your attention to a specific sin. He may be in the process of steering your affections away from the things of the world. God may know that you are on the verge of making a major mistake in your life; perhaps He wants to intensify His relationship with you during this time of decision making. Whatever your circumstances may be, rest assured that God does not do things without a purpose. If He has allowed adversity to enter your world, He has something exciting in store for you!

7

A Not-So-Gentle Reminder

It was a Saturday afternoon about five o'clock when I heard the door slam shut. From the sound of the footsteps, I knew it was my son. He was seven at the time. I put down my pen, walked to his bedroom, and paused outside the door to collect my thoughts. This was the unpleasant part about being a parent—disciplining my children. There was always the nagging fear that the pain I inflicted through discipline would one day turn them against me. But those thoughts were always overshadowed by my fear that they would grow up thinking that they could get by with things, believing that there were no consequences of sin.

When I stepped into Andy's room, he responded as he always did. "Now, wait, I just want to say one thing." It was a stall. He knew it and I knew it, but it was an unavoidable routine we went through every time he got into trouble. If I had not been so grieved by his disobedience, I'm sure I would have viewed the whole scene as comical. Me standing in the doorway prepared to spank him. Him looking around the room for an escape, talking a mile a minute. "Wait, Dad, I just want to say one thing." By this time the inevitability of what was about to take place was beginning to dawn on him. "What would you like to say?" I would always ask. And as tears would begin to fill his eyes, he would blurt out, "Don't spank me!"

There is a second way in which God uses adversity in our lives. He uses it to remind us of His great love; He uses adversity as a form of discipline. As much as we see pain used in discipline in human relationships, you would think that we would readily accept this principle in the context of our spiritual lives as well. Through the years, however, I have observed that this is a difficult concept for many people to accept. They cannot imagine a loving God inflicting pain on His chil-

124

dren. In their minds the concepts of love and pain seem to be diametrically opposed.

But in God's economy, the two go hand in hand, just as they do within human relations. The writer of Hebrews expounds upon this relationship:

> You have forgotten the exhortation which is addressed to you as sons, "My son, do not regard lightly the discipline of the Lord, nor faint when you are reproved by Him; for those whom the Lord loves He disciplines, and He scourges every son whom He receives."   —Hebrews 12:5–6

There is no conflict in the author's mind when it comes to reconciling pain and love. Love necessitates the possibility and even the probability of pain. Notice he says, "He scourges every son whom He receives."

If we think this is strong language in our day, we can only imagine the response this statement must have elicited in the first century. To imply that God "scourges" those He loves must have sent chills down the spines of the early church members. A scourge was a leather whip or a stick used to discipline slaves and criminals. The Romans commonly used a scourge weighted by pieces of bone or metal. This form of punishment was so severe that it was against the law to punish Roman citizens with a scourge. It was not uncommon for men to die as a result of these beatings.

Despite the mental images this term must have conjured up, the author of Hebrews felt at liberty to use it when referring to the discipline of God. This is a very sobering thought—or at least it should be. We are not talking about a little whipping here. This is serious!

The writer of Hebrews knew all too well our tendency not to take the discipline of God as seriously as we should. So he warns us, "Do not regard lightly the discipline of the Lord." In other words, the potential severity of God's discipline should be enough to keep us in line. One of the reasons we fall into sin so easily is that we forget God will discipline us when we step out of bounds. We have forgotten that His complete knowledge of sin and its destructive consequences compels Him to take drastic measures with us. As much as He must disdain using adversity to remind us to live a righteous life, the fact is that He will if He knows that is what it takes.

How Far?

The question that occurs to me as I ponder this awesome doctrine is, "How far is God willing to go?" How much pain dare He inflict? Is there a limit to the adversity He might send? He blinded Paul. He brought Jonah within an inch of his life. I think the answer is that God will do whatever it takes. As much as He must hate pain, He hates sin that much worse. As much as He must despise suffering, He loves us that much more.

For those of us who do not heed this warning of discipline, the writer offers another piece of advice, "Nor faint when you are reproved by Him." The implication here is that when we are undergoing the discipline of God, we will have a tendency to grow discouraged. We will be dangerously open to suggestions by others that cast doubt on the goodness and justice of God. If we are not careful, we will interpret God's discipline for the opposite of what it really is.

We forget that God treats us as sons and daughters. Instead of expecting discipline from our heavenly Father, we are taken by surprise. We misinterpret this act of supreme love. We view as a threat what was intended for our good. But in reality, the discipline of God is a sign of ownership. It serves as the guarantee of our Father-child relationship with God. So the writer says,

> It is for discipline that you endure; God deals with you as with sons; for what son is there whom his father does not discipline? But if you are without discipline, of which all have become partakers, then you are illegitimate children and not sons.
> —Hebrews 12:7–8

By remembering that God will treat us as His children, we can endure the pain of discipline. To forget that is to run the risk of losing all hope, of becoming discouraged, and of giving up altogether.

A Matter of Respect

Now that my kids are grown, I realize more than ever the importance of discipline. The fears I had in those early years really had no substance. Disciplining my children did not cause them to turn against me. On the contrary, I have no doubt that my discipline paved the way to the harmonious relationship we enjoy today. Discipline develops respect. It deepens relationships. The same is true in our relationship with God.

> Furthermore, we had earthly fathers to discipline us, and we respected them; shall we not much rather be subject to the Father of spirits, and live? For they disciplined us for a short time as seemed best to them, but He disciplines us for our good, that we may share His holiness.
> —Hebrews 12:9–10

If we can understand the value of discipline in the context of an earthly father and his children, certainly we can appreciate to some degree the immense value of a heavenly Father who takes the time to discipline His children. All of us have encountered children who have had little or no discipline. Not only are they unpleasant to be around, but their behavior usually gravitates toward those things that are destructive.

I have noticed among the youths of our church that the teenagers who have inclinations toward tobacco, drugs, and alcohol are usually those who come from homes where

129

there is little discipline. Where there is a deficiency in the area of discipline, there is a propensity toward self-destructive behavior. I am not sure I fully understand the relationship between the two, but I have seen this pattern enough to know that the relationship exists.

God is aware of this relationship as well. He knows that unless He disciplines us, chances are that we will allow sin to run its destructive course (see James 1:15). He is all too aware of the ultimate consequences of sin when permitted to go unchecked. His love for us will not let Him sit back and watch our lives be destroyed, so He intervenes with discipline.

Ooops!

Every father knows the pain and embarrassment of realizing he has made the mistake of being too harsh in his discipline or, even worse, of disciplining a child who was not guilty. Yet even with those possibilities always looming over his head, a good father continues the routine of discipline, for the value of discipline is worth the risk of being wrong occasionally.

If we believe an earthly father should

continue disciplining his children—knowing that from time to time his discipline will be unjustified or imperfectly administered—how much more supportive should we be of a perfect, omnipotent, heavenly Father who disciplines His children? If we respected our imperfect earthly fathers when they disciplined us, how much more should we respect our heavenly Father? Whereas our earthly fathers disciplined us according to what they knew, we can be assured that the discipline of our heavenly Father will be perfectly suited to our individual needs.

Sharing His Holiness

There is another major difference between the discipline of our fathers and the discipline of God. This one has to do with purpose. Oftentimes the primary reason we were disciplined by our parents was to make us "behave" or be "good." Sometimes their reasons were selfish; they just did not want to be embarrassed. Our heavenly Father has a different agenda. The writer of Hebrews put it this way:

> But He disciplines us for our good,
> that we may share His holiness. . . . it

> yields the peaceful fruit of righteous-
> ness.   —Hebrews 12:10–11

God's goal in discipline is not simply to make us behave. His purpose is to make us holy, to bring us into conformity with His Son. He wants to build into our experience a hatred for sin similar to His own—a hatred that will cause us to separate ourselves not only from the practice of evil, but from the very appearance of it as well. Through this process, our character will be fine-tuned to reflect the character of Christ Himself. Because God knows us inside and out, He can tailor our discipline in such a way to accomplish just that.

Sorting It Out

When I stood at my son's door prepared to punish him, there was no doubt in his mind what was about to happen. Nor was there any doubt as to why it was about to happen. I always did my best to administer discipline soon after an offense was committed.

The discipline of the Lord is not always as apparent as human discipline. As a result, there is a great deal of confusion in this area. The Lord does not appear in the night to tell us how and why we are going to be disciplined. In fact, at times it seems as if our sin is going unnoticed. Nothing happens! On the other hand, as soon as something bad happens to some believers, they immediately start looking within to see if they can discover some unconfessed sin. As I close this chapter, I want to give you some guidelines to help you identify adversity that is from God as a form of discipline.

1. God wants us to know when we are being disciplined. It does us no good if we are being disciplined but remain unaware of what is going on. What good would it do for a father to spank his child without telling him or her why? Could the father really expect his child's behavior to change if the child was not told why he was being disciplined? Of course not. In the same way, God knows that for discipline to accomplish its desired end, we must be informed.

2. The discipline we incur will be connected in some way to the sin we commit. This point is related to the principle of sowing and reaping. Paul wrote:

> For **whatever** a man sows, **this** he will
> also reap.
> —Galatians 6:7 (emphasis mine)

Notice the italicized words. There is an apparent relationship between what a person *does* and the consequences that follow. When our children would come in later than the curfew we had set for them, Anna and I would discipline them by setting the curfew even earlier the next time. If the children abused their television privileges, they lost those privileges for a time. Discipline is most effective when there is an obvious relationship between the offense and the result.

Some Christian women cannot have children today because they abused their bodies through drug or alcohol abuse or through an immoral lifestyle involving several sexual partners when they were younger. This is the discipline of God. Some Christian men and women have been caught in adultery and have lost their families and careers as a result. This, too, is the discipline of God. When a Christian businessman is caught stealing money from his company and loses his job and reputation, this is the discipline of God.

Jonah tried to run from God, and God stopped him from running. Israel was not faithful to God in the land He gave them, so He disciplined them by taking them out

134

of the land. David destroyed Bathsheba's family through his treachery and adultery. God destroyed his family through the treachery of his son, Absalom.

3. Spiritual insensitivity can hinder a believer's ability to see that God is administering discipline. I talk to people all the time who are mad at God for the adversity He has allowed into their lives. As we talk, I discover that they have not been walking with God. They are involved in all kinds of sin. And yet they cannot see the connection. They come to me hoping I can press a "magic button" and relieve them of their pain.

God is not about to let up on a believer until He has accomplished what He has set out to do. If a man or woman refuses to give in, God will just turn up the heat. Remember, His ultimate goal for you and me is not ease, comfort, or pleasure. It is conformity to the image of His Son. And He is willing to go to great lengths to accomplish His purpose.

The writer of Hebrews summed it up well when he wrote,

> All discipline for the moment seems
> not to be joyful, but sorrowful; yet to
> those who have been trained by it, af-

terwards it yields the peaceful fruit of righteousness.   —Hebrews 12:11

Saying that discipline "seems not to be joyful" is putting it mildly. Discipline is something we despise for the moment. Like my son at age seven, we all look for a place to run, an excuse with which to stall. No one enjoys it. Yet those of us who have endured it know that the fruit it produces and the pain from which it ultimately spares us makes it worth the agony.

Are you experiencing the discipline of God in your life? Are you suffering from the consequences of sin? Where would you be today if God had allowed you to continue getting away with your rebellion and disobedience? As you look around at others who continue to "get away" with their sin, do you really envy them? Or can you understand that God's love for you moved Him to stop you dead in your tracks and turn your attention back toward Him?

It is true that "all discipline for the moment seems not to be joyful, but sorrowful." But if you will let go and allow God to finish His work, you will experience the "peaceful fruit of righteousness" He has promised to those whom He loves.

8

A Self-Examination

Linda noticed that her bedroom floor made an annoying creaking sound when she walked over a particular area. For the first few weeks she tried to ignore it. Her condominium was brand-new, and she assumed that the noise was simply the result of settling. As the weeks went on, however, the noise grew worse and worse. Finally she called the builder and asked him to take a look. He didn't seem very concerned. "Every new building has its noises," he assured her. But just to be on the safe side he pulled back the carpet and cut a hole in the floor to take a closer look. To his surprise he discovered that the beams designed to join the floor with the supporting wall had been cut too short. They were just barely long enough to make it to the support beam. Not only that, nothing had been done to fasten the floor beams to the support.

The creaking noise Linda had heard was the sound of the floor beams slowly sliding closer to the edge of their supports. Had the problem not been discovered, her floor would have eventually caved in. A crew went to work immediately to remedy the situation. Again, to be on the safe side, the builder had every unit checked. The same problem was found in three other buildings as well. Had it not been for the annoying creak in Linda's floor, she would have never discovered the builder's error. The creak in her floor may have saved her life.

Looking Beneath the Surface

Oftentimes God will allow annoying creaks to occur in the floor of our lives—circumstances or people that are a constant annoyance to us. But as in the case of Linda, these annoyances are God's way of drawing our attention to potentially dangerous blind spots, habits, or emotional baggage from our past. Through them, we are forced to do some serious self-examination. This is the third purpose for which God permits the believer to experience adversity.

In chapter 6 we discussed the fact that God sends adversity to gain our undivided attention. There is some overlap between that principle and the one we will be discussing in this chapter. The primary difference is that in this case we are not talking about a believer who has grown spiritually insensitive or who is running from God. This principle applies to those who are committed to doing the will of God. It presupposes a desire to grow. In chapter 6 we focused on believers who were aware of sin or rebellion but were unwilling to do anything about it. The principle we are examining in this chapter goes a step further.

Step by Step

Spiritual growth is much like physical growth. There are stages of development. Each stage brings with it new expectations and greater freedom. No one would expect a newborn baby to walk. Yet we would be very concerned about a twelve-year-old who was still crawling. We do not think less of a two-year-old because he or she cannot read.

Adversity
removes the
cloak of
"what we are
supposed to be"
to reveal the
truth of what
we are.

But we expect adults to have developed some skill in this area.

Spiritual growth is the same way. God's expectations for new Christians are different from those He has for people who have been Christians for many years. Don't misunderstand what I am saying. God's moral standard is the same for every believer. What I am referring to here are things such as character development, discernment, and the surrender of rights and possessions. These are areas of the spiritual life that take a lifetime to develop. Nature clearly demonstrates that the things that grow the strongest usually grow slowly. Only weeds and toadstools pop up overnight.

When people become Christians, they are forced to address certain issues almost immediately: things such as how to handle old friends and how to explain to family members what has happened to them. Usually they are challenged to deal with some sinful habits as well. For the most part, these things are obvious. It does not take a great deal of insight to point them out.

As time goes on, however, and these surface issues are taken care of, God sees fit to begin working on those things that are not so obvious. He is not satisfied with simply calling us to task for our acts of disobedience. He wants to get at the root: pride, prejudices, selfishness, materialism. On and on the list goes to include anger, bitterness, jealousy, grudges, and a judgmental spirit— the kinds of things that seep out subtly in our conversation, our quiet remarks, and our "humor." Along with these, He desires to heal emotional wounds we may be carrying, such as hurts, fears, and insecurities that are the result of things that have happened in our past. He wants to weed out wrong attitudes. He wants to bring to our attention incorrect ideas we were taught as children, things that have caused us to misinterpret the actions of others. He wants to correct our thinking about ourselves as well as our perception of Him. These issues are not dealt with by simply confessing sin. It takes more.

Making Us Aware

Often, we are unaware that these problems even exist. So God sees fit to allow a little adversity into our lives to motivate us to do some self-examination. The winds of adversity blow off the surface issues and force us to cope with things on a deeper level. God may work through a conflict between you and a friend. He may use your spouse. God may use finances or even one of your children.

God knows how to get our attention. And eventually we become aware of annoying creaks in the floor of our lives. Things quit going as smoothly as they had been. Life is not as easy as it once was. When the structure of life begins falling apart, it may be God's way of saying, "It is time to take a long, hard look within. It is time you discovered what really drives you and causes you to react the way you do."

This is never any fun. It is not the kind of spiritual growth we look forward to or pray for. But during these times of self-examination, we make the greatest strides forward in our relationship with God and others. During these periods of self-examination, God is able to get at the cause of much of our inconsistency and self-will. During these times, we see ourselves for what we really are and not what we pretend to be. If we allow God to reveal all He wishes to reveal, permanent change takes place.

Examine Yourselves!

The apostle Paul commanded the members of the Corinthian church to examine themselves. They were experiencing an unusually high rate of sickness and death among their fellowship. Paul made it clear that this adversity was sent to reveal something about the character of those involved in the church there in Corinth. They were divisive, gluttonous, and disrespectful of the Lord's table (see 1 Cor. 11:19–30). To get their attention, God began disciplining them by striking them with illness and even death! Paul responded by saying,

> But let a man examine himself.
> —1 Corinthians 11:28

In other words, "Take an inquisitive look inside and discover what is driving you to such disrespectful behavior." God was not about to allow such confusion to continue, so He sent them some physical ailment to move them back on track.

God does not want negative elements from the past to lie around in our lives and cause us to deteriorate. We are the temple of the Holy Spirit. He wants us to be clean and us-

144

able vessels. There is no reason to allow the rubbish of the past to remain in our lives for years and years. When He knows we are able to deal with it, He moves to bring it to our attention. And as painful as it may seem, from God's perspective it is always worthwhile.

Mr. Right

I was talking with a young woman from our singles department who had just been dumped by her boyfriend. She was devastated. Sharla was sure Ben was the "one." She had been praying for God's best since she was in high school. And for some time she felt as if he was the answer to her prayers. They had talked about marriage and even looked at rings. Then with very little warning, he broke off the relationship completely.

As we talked, I felt free to dig a little. I asked her many questions about the relationship. The more we talked, the more transparent she became. She finally admitted that she had been the aggressive one in the relationship. She had pushed Ben, and he finally hit the road. This was painful for Sharla to admit. But with tears in her eyes she admitted that it was her fault he had broken up with her.

Things were going well, so I took the liberty to dig just a little bit deeper. "Why do you think you were so pushy?" I asked.

She shrugged, "I don't know. I have always been that way."

"Always?" I asked.

"As far back as I can remember. My brothers always told me I was 'bossy.' And now that I think about it, they were right."

As we continued to talk, I noticed some familiar patterns in her early family life. Sharla came from a home where a great deal was expected from her. These high expectations coupled with a lack of affection from either of her parents had produced in her an aggressive spirit. She had learned to perform for acceptance. She always did well at whatever she attempted to do. Her reward, however, was not Dad's warm arm of love around her shoulders. Instead she was congratulated with a handshake or some sort of monetary reward.

Eventually, the focus of the conversation shifted away from her and Ben. I began to help Sharla unravel some emotions she had been struggling with for years: the desire to be loved for who she was rather than what she could do; feelings of loneliness and isolation; an inability to wait on the Lord. She was quick to see the connection between these emotional patterns and the environment in which she was reared.

In the months that followed I watched God change Sharla. Her cold aggressiveness disappeared. She became more sensitive toward and accepting of others. Later she admitted to a friend that her breakup with Ben was the best thing that ever happened to her. And I would have to agree, for it was through that tragedy that God allowed her to see a layer of immaturity He was ready to remove.

Why the Pain?

One might wonder if bringing this type of thing to the surface is really worth the emotional anguish. I will admit that sometimes it does not seem worthwhile. But we must remember that God's goal for us is spiritual maturity. The apostle Paul said we are to "grow up in all aspects into Him" (Eph. 4:15). Besides the fact that it is God's will, there are other practical benefits to dealing with conflicts from the past.

The most obvious one is that it protects future relationships from being inundated by the eventual negative overflow from these unresolved conflicts. As much as we may try to suppress it, the undealt-with sin from our past will eventually emerge. It may take a while, but it will seep through the cracks. And usually our families suffer. Therefore, the sooner God reveals these things to us, the better. Every major family counseling session I have been involved in centered on problems that stemmed from some family member's past. Because of this, I begin almost every session with questions about early family life.

Putting It Off

The longer we allow these things to go unsettled, the greater their negative potential; the deeper the roots, the more painful the excavation process and the greater our resistance to let them go. This is why God keeps the pressure on us. He knows that if He lets up, we will return to our old ways. We need incentive to look within. Nobody wants to face what is really on the inside. But until we get a good dose of reality, we will make very few changes. The winds of adversity blow away our careful disguises. Adversity removes the cloak of "what we are supposed to be" to reveal the truth of what we are. And as painful as it may be, it

148

is only then that God can complete what He has begun.

A Regular Checkup

Getting a medical checkup is a good idea because it almost guarantees that any threat to health can be detected early before it endangers one's life. Those people who are afraid of what the doctor might find and therefore put off an examination are the ones who get themselves into trouble. It is foolish to ignore the warnings the body sends. It is even more foolish to ignore God's warnings.

Had Linda not called the builder to check her floor, there is no telling what might have happened or how serious the damage might have been—to her and even to others. In the same way, if we don't respond to the adversities that come our way by crying out to the Lord for insight, we, too, run a great risk. Through the winds of adversity, God wants to reveal the hidden things: the characteristics and patterns of behavior that have the potential to ruin future relationships, damage your testimony, and one day destroy your family. Don't run. Don't try to ignore what God is doing. By putting God off, you only hurt yourself.

Looking within may be a painful experience. But remember, whatever you find there, no matter how devastatingly painful it might be, Jesus Himself is there to help you carry that burden to the cross and deal with it once and for all. He has your best interest in mind. He knows that pain sometimes paves the path to complete healing and restoration of the inner man.

In her book *Affliction*, Edith Schaeffer, wife of the late Francis Schaeffer, includes a prayer for those who are struggling with the pain so often involved in the process of sanctification:

> Please let me come out of this closer to You, more mature as Your child, with a skimming off of some of the impurities which are spoiling the reflection of Your face as You look at me.

If you are willing to allow God to surface those hidden and ever-so-subtle inconsistencies and hurts in your life, and if you are willing to cope with them as He directs, you will indeed emerge from the whole process closer to Christ, more mature as His child, and with far greater potential to be a reflection of the love of God.

9

A Humbling Experience

During my thirty-six years of ministry, I have seen many talented preachers come and go. They explode on the scene like sprinters off the starting blocks. They are invited to the right churches. They are introduced to all the right people. They gather letters of recommendation from the superstars of the evangelical world. They are heralded as the next Billy Graham or Spurgeon. But after a few years in the limelight, they drop out of sight. Some are never heard from again.

Some of these men were personal friends of mine. Others I knew only from a distance.

But of the ones I had opportunity to know or minister with, one thing about them stands out in my mind above everything else: they all had a touch of arrogance in their demeanor. I am not talking about overt conceit. In most cases it was more subtle than that.

These promising young preachers suffered from the same ailment that afflicts most men and women who spend too much time in the spotlight. I like to think of it as spiritual amnesia. Instead of forgetting who they are, however, they begin to forget the Source of all they are. They forget that God is the voice and that they are simply the mouthpiece. They lose sight of the fact that God could turn off the flow at any time, leaving them high and dry, not only in their spiritual lives, but in their careers as well.

As we would have these men in our home or spend time with them at a conference or convention, it became obvious to Anna and me that they had begun to believe their own press reports. They had taken the applause of man too seriously. An unguarded word or a critical glance revealed to us what would later prove to be true. Lurking beneath the surface of their polished sermons and heartrending prayers was a sinister force slowly chipping away at their foundations. It was a gradual process that in many cases resulted in the destruction of what had taken years to accomplish.

Another Shooting Star

Ben Hillary is a perfect example. Ben was a football star in high school and college. He was outgoing and friendly, and he really had a heart for God. He gave up what promised to be a successful business career in order to become a minister of the gospel. After seminary, he took a church in Florida where he was recognized immediately as a gifted preacher and teacher. His church began to grow by leaps and bounds. After just a short time as pastor, he was heralded as one of the most outstanding young preachers in America.

But something happened. He grew confused as to who really deserved the applause. Pride crept in. It was as if he never got off the football field. He began playing to the crowd. He grew dependent upon the praise and acceptance of men. His twisted perspective began to affect his ability to make decisions. Soon everything he did hinged upon what everybody else would think. After a series of unwise choices, he was asked to leave his church. That was the last I heard of Ben.

God hates pride. It was pride that made sin a reality in God's creation. And it was pride that brought sin into this world:

> The fear of the LORD is to hate evil;
> Pride and arrogance and the evil way
> And the perverted mouth, I hate.
> —Proverbs 8:13

God hates pride so much that He is willing to allow adversity into the lives of His children in order to root it out. As we will see, God has such a disdain for pride that He is even willing to go so far as to send adversity to keep pride from ever becoming a problem. And so the fourth reason God allows adversity in our lives is to conquer our pride.

Why Me?

In his second letter to the Corinthian church Paul spoke of his "thorn in the flesh." Apparently this was some form of adversity—probably physical—that caused him much discomfort and anxiety. This adver-

154

sity drove him to his knees and caused him to do some serious self-examination. After begging the Lord three times to remove his thorn, he discovered something about himself. During this time of intense soul-searching, God revealed to Paul the reason for this "thorn."

Paul described it this way:

> And because of the surpassing greatness of the revelations, for this reason, to keep me from exalting myself, there was given me a thorn in the flesh, a messenger of Satan to buffet me—**to keep me from exalting myself!**
> —2 Corinthians 12:7 (emphasis mine)

God, foreseeing the possibility of Paul's becoming proud, allowed a messenger of Satan to "buffet" him. The thorn in flesh was God's way of doing some preventive maintenance. It was His way of assuring that Paul's popularity and special spiritual privilege would not cause him to think more highly of himself than he ought. God knew Paul's potential for His kingdom. And He was going to do everything He could to ensure that Paul's ego did not get in the way of his ministry.

Recognizing Your Potential

God knows your potential for His kingdom. He knows what kind of influence you could have. Most believers underestimate their spiritual potential. They think, What could I do for God? He doesn't need me. But my friend, it is not a matter of God's needing you. The point is that God has chosen you to represent Him within your sphere of influence. Your sphere may be your home. It may be your office or the crew you work with. Size is not important. You may be the one person in this world someone at work will listen to. And if you are the difference between heaven and hell for one soul, you have tremendous potential!

Another area of spiritual potential is often overlooked. We tend to focus on the public work of the kingdom. But a private side to the work of God's kingdom is equally (if not more) important—prayer. All of us have great potential through prayer, for the essence of the spiritual life is the struggle occurring in heavenly places (see Eph. 6:12). Prayer is the believer's means of participating in this heavenly battle. Only heaven will reveal the real spiritual heroes. I believe there will be many highly honored people who remained unknown in this life, yet who faithfully supported those in public ministry with prayer.

The Downside

God is not the only One who recognizes your potential. Satan sees it as well. He loves to take a person's success and use it against him or her. He takes great joy in convincing preachers, teachers, and singers that they really are as "wonderful" as people say. He specializes in developing a haughty and critical spirit in those who see prayer as their calling, people who say, "I bet the preacher doesn't even pray as much as I do." He is an expert at confusing counselors as to the source of their insight. Satan knows that nothing forfeits a man's or woman's usefulness to God like pride. No other sin neutralizes a ministry as quickly as pride.

God used Jonah in spite of his rebellion. He used David in spite of his immorality. He even used Abraham after he expressed a lack of faith and lied to Pharaoh. But whenever you find a man in Scripture who gets puffed up with pride, that spells the beginning of the end.

Nebuchadnezzar is a perfect example. One

day he was the king of Babylon; the next day he was driven out as a crazy man (see Dan. 4:30–33). Why? Pride. It was Solomon's pride that eventually destroyed his rule as well. Pride will cause God to put a man or woman on the shelf more quickly than anything else, for God refuses to share His glory with anyone.

> Pride goes before destruction, And a haughty spirit before stumbling.
> —Proverbs 16:18

> God is opposed to the proud, but gives grace to the humble.   —James 4:6

A believer who becomes proud is living in opposition to God. The Christian life is designed to be a life of dependency. When pride moves into a life, it slowly wears down the sense of dependency, for the essence of pride is self-sufficiency. By allowing pride to creep into one's personality, a believer develops an attitude toward life that is diametrically opposed to what God intends. God does not help the proud; He does not encourage the proud; He does not assist the proud; He resists the proud.

158

It's No Wonder

In light of our potential for the kingdom and the devastating effect pride has on our relationship with our heavenly Father, it is understandable why God would go to painfully great lengths to keep us humble. Imagine how much God must have loved the apostle Paul. He allowed him to pen half of the New Testament!

Yet He also afflicted Paul with a thorn in the flesh that stayed with him his entire life. The only way to reconcile such privilege with such pain is to realize how much God hates pride—and in Paul's case, even the potential of pride.

If God was willing to head off Paul's pride at the pass through adversity, is it unreasonable to assume that He would do the same for us? Is not our potential for God's kingdom as important to our Lord as Paul's? Is He any less interested in having an intimate relationship with us than He was with the apostle? Of course not. Therefore, the adversity you are struggling with right now may be God's way of taming your pride.

Think about it this way. If you knew that your pride had the potential to hinder you from being all God wanted you to be, would you be willing to ask God to do whatever was necessary to keep it in check? Well, if the thought of praying that kind of prayer causes you to shudder, I have some good news and some bad news. The good news is that you do not need to ask God to send something into your life to tame your pride. The bad news is that He will probably do so on His own initiative!

The tragedy is that some people are smart enough to weasel their way through or around the adversity God intends to use. Through their own ingenuity and determination, they manipulate things in such a way as to temporarily bypass God's plan for keeping them humble. This may work in the short run, but nobody outsmarts or outmaneuvers God! For a while these people are able to continue functioning or even ministering as if nothing has changed. But slowly, what is true privately begins to surface publicly. People begin to notice a change, a lack of power, self-conceit, and sometimes, without their even knowing it, God shelves them.

The Story of Sheila

There was a very talented woman in our church several years ago who was particularly good with young people. The kids in our church were drawn to her as to no one else I have ever seen. Her congenial personality along with her communication skills made her an excellent teacher and role model. But as is true so often with talented people she had a tendency to rely a little too much on the praises of others. I noticed a shift in her attitude toward her work and ministry. The approval of others became more important than the unspoken approval of God. Pride began to take over.

As this transformation was taking place, I watched as God tried twice to humble Sheila. His first effort was through one of her children. Her oldest daughter was born with a physical condition that caused Sheila a great deal of public embarrassment. Instead of embracing her daughter's problem and making a commitment to love her regardless of the cost socially and financially, Sheila rejected Mindy. She criticized her publicly for things that were beyond Mindy's control. Eventually Sheila worked out a situation in which others would care for Mindy until she could care for herself. And all the time Sheila justified her behavior by pointing to the significance of her ministry.

A few years later Sheila's husband lost

his job. As a result, he lost his confidence as well. He went for some time without work and finally took a job with the city. Both the type of work he did and the salary he brought home were not what Sheila was used to. Once again she dodged what I believe was another attempt by God to humble her. Instead of supporting her husband in a time when he really needed her, she left him.

I have not seen Sheila for quite some time. After leaving her husband, she went into business for herself. Not long afterward, she dropped all ministry responsibilities at the church. The last thing I heard about her was that she was doing well in her business but was totally away from the Lord. A success in the eyes of the world, she is far from that in the eyes of God.

Painful Love

Just as God had big plans for the apostle Paul, He has big plans for you. There are unsaved people only you can reach. There are hurting saints only you can comfort. And God is not about to allow pride to diminish your potential if He can help it.

Like Sheila, you can resist. But you will hurt only yourself. As painful as it may be,

162

adversity is an expression of God's love. By working to conquer your pride, God works to preserve your potential and your life. Pride is always followed by destruction of some kind. It could be the destruction of your family, your career, or your very life.

Are you struggling with adversity of some kind? Could it be that God has allowed this hardship in your life in order to conquer your pride? If so, are you willing to thank Him? Not for the adversity itself, but for His great love and concern for you and your family. If you can praise Him with sincerity of heart for His active concern and involvement in your life, you have taken a giant step toward advancing through your adversity!

10

The Power of Weakness

One of my favorite Old Testament narratives is the story of David and Goliath. From the way the writer describes this incident, an outsider would have found the whole thing somewhat comical. It seems that every morning the Israelites would line up on the hillside for battle. Just as they were ready to do battle with the Philistines, Goliath would stroll down into the valley. Standing there dressed for battle, with his shieldbearer by his side, he would shout at the Israelite army and dare them to come and get him. At that point the entire Israelite army would turn around and run back to camp (see 1 Sam. 17:1–24).

165

Apparently this pattern of events had been going on for some time when David appeared on the scene. After a round or two with his brothers, he gathered five stones and went down into the valley to challenge Goliath. Again, to anyone watching from the hillside, this must have been amusing. Imagine—David and his sling going against the giant and his weapons of war. But to everyone's surprise (not the least of which was Goliath) David emerged the victor.

Many great lessons can be drawn from this familiar narrative. And many stirring sermons have been preached concerning David's faith and courage. But for just a moment let's look at this story from God's perspective. In doing so, we gain great insight into the mind of God and discover another way in which He uses adversity in our lives.

Why did God choose to use David in this encounter with Goliath? He was untrained, ill-prepared, inexperienced, and young. Humanly speaking, he had nothing going for him. There were thousands of well-trained Israelite soldiers present who would have been far more likely candidates. Yet God chose David. Why?

What If . . . ?

Imagine for just a moment that you are the bystander I spoke of a couple of paragraphs ago. You are sitting on the hillside watching all that is taking place. You see Goliath coming down into the valley on his daily run. Then you notice a stirring among the Israelite soldiers. A cheer goes up from their ranks as one of their own takes up his sword and shield and charges down into the valley. Although this fellow is not as big as Goliath, he is certainly no wimp, either. As he positions himself to fight, it becomes apparent that this man has seen many battles and has probably faced great odds before.

Then suddenly the two warriors lunge at each other. For several minutes it looks as if this valiant Israelite warrior has met his match. But then, faster than you could bat an eye, our hero performs an incredible maneuver that catches Goliath off guard. As the giant struggles to regain his advantage, the Israelite thrusts his sword through the Philistine's breastplate and falls with him to the ground. For a minute the two men struggle together on the ground. But the blow proves to be fatal, and soon Goliath's body lies lifeless. The Israelite soldier slowly

Your biggest
weakness
is God's
greatest
opportunity.

stands, picks up the giant's sword, and with one swoop separates the Philistine's head from his body. The men of the Israelite army cheer wildly as their enemies flee.

Exciting, huh? But not all that surprising. We have seen the underdog win before. Besides, Goliath made a tactical error, and the Israelite took advantage of it. No big deal. We could chalk the whole thing up to military skill and leave God out of the picture completely. God did not choose to send a soldier for that very reason. He chose a young shepherd instead. He looked for someone who seemed to have not even the slightest chance of success. Someone who would be completely dependent upon Him. An instrument through which He could demonstrate His mighty power in such a way as to get credit for it. When David slew Goliath that day, there was no doubt in his mind who delivered the giant into his hands (see 1 Sam. 17:37). And there was no doubt in anyone else's mind, either.

God's Choice

The point is simply this: the greater the odds, the better for God. Our heavenly Father gets far more attention and thus more glory when He works through persons the world considers weak. The apostle Paul put it this way:

> But God has chosen the foolish things of the world to shame the wise, and God has chosen the weak things of the world to shame the things which are strong, and the base things of the world and the despised, God has chosen, the things that are not, that He might nullify the things that are, that no man should boast before God.
> —1 Corinthians 1:27–29

Look at that second phrase. God chooses to use the weak things of the world. He does not have to. That is His choice. When He uses what is weak, His power and might are that much more evident.

So how does all of this fit into our discussion of adversity? One of the reasons God allows adversity into our lives is to cause us to rely on His strength instead of our own. In doing so, He perfects His power in us (see 2 Cor. 12:9). Relying on His power manifests His sufficiency to us and to all those who are familiar with our situation. David's victory was a source of rejoicing and encouragement to the entire nation of Israel. And so it is when God works through one of His children in spite of the individual's weakness.

Handicaps

Adversities always handicap us in some way. They either slow us down physically or drain us emotionally and mentally. Adversities keep us from functioning at 100 percent. Our minds get divided. Our energy level is low. And even the simplest tasks become major ordeals. Jobs that once took a couple of hours now take all day. Our tempers shorten. And the least little thing irritates us to no end.

Recently I was having to deal with a sensitive family situation. My stepfather is blind and unable to care for himself any longer. This was becoming a terrible strain on my mother. In spite of the pressure that having him at home was placing on her, she did not want me to put John in a nursing home. Back and forth we went. Finally, after much prayer and discussion, I put John in the nicest nursing home I could find. After visiting him one Saturday, my mother decided they were not taking care of him the way they should, so she packed his things and brought him back home. Poor John. For a while there he did not know from week to week where he would be living.

I can remember sitting down to study and struggling to concentrate on my work. My mind kept wandering; I would find myself staring out the window, thinking about my mom and John. It killed me to see her suffering. And yet I did not want to force her to do something against her will. The incident served to handicap me mentally and emotionally.

That is the nature of all adversity. It robs us of the resources we need to function properly. Areas of strength become our greatest weaknesses. Adversity is always unexpected and unwelcomed. It is an intruder and a thief. And yet in the hands of God, adversity becomes the means through which His supernatural power is demonstrated.

Perfect Power

The apostle Paul certainly understood this principle. After asking God three times to remove his thorn in the flesh, Paul finally received an answer. It was not what he expected. God told him flatly that He would not remove the thorn. He would, however, supply the extra strength Paul needed to carry out the work he had been called to do.

> And He has said to me, "My grace is sufficient for you, for power is perfected in weakness." Most gladly, therefore, I will rather boast about my weaknesses, that the power of Christ may dwell in me. . . . for when I am weak, then I am strong.
> —2 Corinthians 12:9–10

Like all of us, Paul wanted his circumstances to be right. So that is how he prayed: "Lord, get rid of this thorn." But God wanted Paul to live with a handicap. It was His will that Paul remain weak. But not for weakness's sake. God's purpose was to weaken Paul's dependence on his own strength, his own wisdom, his own intellect. God wanted Paul to minister and live out of his weakness, not his strength. This is the idea behind the phrase "power is perfected in weakness."

The term perfected does not mean perfect in a moral sense, as in perfect versus imperfect; the idea here is that of being "completed" or "fulfilled." God was giving Paul a general principle. According to this principle, the weaker something is, the greater its need for strength. When what is weak is finally strengthened, the presence of renewed strength is more noticeable by comparison. One of the best ways for God to show forth His power is to manifest it through an otherwise weak or handicapped vessel. For this reason, God allows adversity to enter our experience: not for the purpose of making us weak and incapable of going on with our lives, but for the purpose of enabling us by His strength to do what otherwise would be impossible.

A Painful Priority

From God's perspective, it was more important for Paul to experience supernatural power than it was for him to live a pain-free, adversity-free life. The closer you look at Paul's life, the more difficult that is to accept. He was stoned and left for dead, shipwrecked, beaten, bitten by a snake, and finally imprisoned—all for Christ's sake. When all was said and done, Paul's response was this:

> Therefore I am well content with
> weaknesses, with insults, with dis-

tresses, with persecutions, with difficulties, for Christ's sake; for when I
am weak, then I am strong.
—2 Corinthians 12:10

I have seen men and women emerge from far less strenuous circumstances than Paul's full of anger and hostility. They were mad at God for what He did to them. But not Paul. Why? Because he recognized that what God allowed to be done to him was simply prepa-ration for what He wanted to do for him. As Paul grew more and more dependent upon the Lord for strength, it became second na-ture to him. His faith in Christ grew to the point that he could say with all sincerity, "I am well content with weaknesses."

The whole idea of being content with weakness contradicts the messages society sends us. In an age of power lunches and power ties, it is unusual for people to get very excited about living in a state of weak-ness. But upon examining the life of the apostle Paul, one hardly gets the impression that he was a weak man. On the contrary, he debated against Christ's apostles over the question of gentile salvation, and he won! He spent his life preaching in the most hos-tile of circumstances. He planted churches throughout the major cities of Asia Minor and in the port cities along the Aegean Sea. Paul trained the first pastors and elders of these early congregations. And to top it all off, he wrote half of the New Testament!

I don't know what you think, but that certainly doesn't sound like a weak man to me. If Paul had been a businessman, he would have been extremely successful. He knew how to set goals and accomplish them. He understood the principles involved in motivating people. He was a mover and a shaker.

So how do we reconcile Paul's claim to weakness with his amazing accomplishments? Simple, the answer is in the phrase, "when I am weak, then I am strong." A paraphrase of his comment would go something like this: "When I, Paul, in and of my own strength, am weak, then I, Paul, relying on the power of Christ in me, become strong, capable of whatever the Lord requires of me, full of energy and zeal to accomplish His will."

In Search of the Weak

God wants to work through our weaknesses in the same way He worked through the apostle Paul's. You may have been born with characteristics you consider weaknesses.

Or you may have been born into a family that did not provide you with the things you think are necessary for success. Perhaps a recent tragedy or illness has left you wondering about your usefulness or self-worth.

If any of these situations sound familiar to you, rejoice! You are just the type of person God is looking for. He wants people through whom He can show off His mighty power, people who know their weaknesses and are willing to allow Him to control and direct their lives. God is looking for men and women who are willing to take on challenges too difficult for them to handle, trusting Him to carry the load. He wants people who understand from experience what Paul meant when he wrote, "My [God's] grace is sufficient for you." Believers who grow accustomed to weakness, but who draw daily upon the sufficiency and power of Christ!

More times than I can remember I have faced challenges that I knew were beyond my abilities to cope with them. I have suffered rejection from men I thought were my best friends. There have been occasions when I have hurt so deeply and cried so intensely that I told God I was ready to die. But in the midst of my pity parties, as I rehearsed for the heavenly Father what I could and could not do, He has always sent a gentle reminder: "Charles, I was not interested in your strength and your ability when I called you. And I am still not interested in them now. What I want to know is, are you available? If so, then let's go. For My grace is sufficient."

I want you to think about something at this point. Your biggest weakness is God's greatest opportunity. Instead of complaining and begging God to change your circumstances, why not ask Him to fill that void with His strength? God has allowed adversity into your life to loosen your dependence on your own strength. It is His desire that you learn to live in dependence on Him for those things you lack. As you grow more and more accustomed to this arrangement, you will actually begin to sense contentment. His power will be perfected in you. And as you make yourself available, His power will be demonstrated through you to the lives of others. And with the apostle Paul you will be able to boast in your weakness. For when you are weak, then He is strong!

I I

Faithful Is He Who Called You

You may have heard it said that a person does not really know who his friends are until the bottom drops out. I think there is great truth to that. All of us have experienced the pain of discovering that people we thought would be faithful—no matter what— were simply "fair-weather friends." You know, friends whose loyalty hinges upon the climate of the circumstances. As long as the relationship is enjoyable, they are with you all the way. But when it begins to demand some sacrifice on their part, they are hard to find. The ultimate measure of friends is not where they stand in times of comfort and

179

convenience, but where they stand in times of challenge and controversy. That being the case, apart from adversity of some kind, we would never know who our faithful friends really are.

In the same way, we will never know in a personal way the faithfulness of Christ apart from adversity. As a result, our faith in Him would never increase. It would remain static. One of the primary reasons God allows us to face adversity is so that He can demonstrate His faithfulness and in turn increase our faith. If you are a believer, you have made a decision to trust Christ with your eternal destiny. But you will not experience His faithfulness in that particular area until you die. God wants more from you and for you than simple intellectual acknowledgment of His faithfulness. It is His will that you experience it now.

If our lives are free from pain, turmoil, and sorrow, our knowledge of God will remain purely academic. Our relationship with Him could be compared to that of a great-great-grandfather about whom we have heard stories, yet never met personally. We would have great admiration, but no intimacy, no fellowship. There would always be a sense of distance and mystery.

That is not the kind of relationship God wants with His children. Through the death of Christ, God has opened the way for us to have direct access to Him. He went to great lengths to clear the way so that nothing stands between Him and His children. There is potential now for intimacy between us and our Creator. Christ went so far as to say that we are His friends (see John 15:14–15).

God is in the process of engineering circumstances through which He can reveal Himself to each of us. And both history as well as our personal testimonies bear witness to the fact that it is in times of adversity that we come to a greater realization of God's incredible faithfulness to us.

For Example . . .

Imagine how Noah's comprehension of God's faithfulness must have been increased after having been delivered through the Flood. Think about how David's faith was increased through his battle with the lion and the bear that came to steal his sheep. I can't imagine what must have been running through Gideon's mind when God told him he had too many soldiers and he had to get rid of most of them (see Judg. 7)! But after the victory, his faith soared. God used the Red Sea and Jericho to demonstrate His faithfulness to Israel. He used Lot's selfishness in Abraham's life. And on and on we could go. In every case, adversity was the means through which God revealed His faithfulness to His servants.

The psalmist expressed it this way:

> I sought the LORD, and He answered
> me,
> And delivered me from all my
> fears. . . .
> This poor man cried and the LORD
> heard him,
> And saved him out of all his troubles.
> The angel of the LORD encamps
> around those who fear Him,
> And rescues them. . . .
> Many are the afflictions of the righteous;
> But the LORD delivers him out of them
> all.
> —Psalm 34:4, 6–7, 19

Here is the description of someone who is experiencing the faithfulness of God. An experience that would be impossible apart from "fear," "troubles," and "afflictions."

Notice that the writer is not depressed or angry with God. On the contrary, the mood of the psalm is very positive and upbeat. It is a psalm of praise and thanksgiving. Where there is adversity, there is always great potential for praise. The most elaborate celebrations described in the Scriptures always followed an event in which God demonstrated His faithfulness through adversity.

Think back to the last time you genuinely praised the Lord for something He had done. Were the events leading up to your excitement touched by adversity or conflict of some kind? More than likely they were. God's faithfulness through adversity is usually the catalyst for praise. And in the process, faith is stretched and strengthened.

My Latest Cause for Praise

The series of events leading to my most recent experience of praise were full of adversity. For the past week I have been involved in a continuing dialogue with a young lady who had made the decision to end her pregnancy through abortion. She knew it was wrong, but the thought of telling her family and friends was overwhelming. Besides, she had just started a new career, and a baby did not fit into her immediate plans. I met with her and her boyfriend for about an hour and got nowhere. The evening after we had talked, they told a mutual friend that they did not appreciate my trying to scare them.

After several days of not knowing which direction they were heading, I finally got word that the young woman decided to go ahead and have her baby. She called and apologized for her attitude and even thanked me for my help. I have been praising God for His faithfulness ever since. It is not that He was any less faithful before, but by allowing me to see and experience His faithfulness in action, my faith is increased.

In the Real World

Unfortunately, things do not always work out so well. Sometimes circumstances don't work out at all as we'd like. People we pray for die. Husbands leave their wives and never come back. Children wreck and ruin their lives in spite of the influence of godly parents. Businesses go bankrupt. Christians lose their jobs. And thousands of women do have abortions.

But God is no less faithful in these events than He is in the others. His faithfulness, however, takes a different form. Nevertheless, many Christians are quick to doubt God when adversities are not resolved the way they deem appropriate. As a result, they doubt God. Some become angry and turn their back on Him completely. I cannot tell you how many men and women I have counseled who lived for years in rebellion toward God over this very issue. God did not do things the way they thought He should, so they wrote Him off as unfaithful and walked away.

God is always faithful to His promises. Nowhere, however, did He promise to always work things out the way we think they should be. If that were the case, He would be no more than a magic genie. God's ways are not our ways. And in the same vein, His goals are oftentimes not our goals. But He is always faithful.

Faithful Just the Same

God's faithfulness does not always take the form of deliverance from adversity. Many times God demonstrates His faithfulness by sustaining us through adversity. Take, for instance, a man marooned on a deserted island. As he explores the island looking for food, he discovers a speedboat washed up on shore. Upon further examination he finds that the tank is full of gas. He cranks the engine, and away he goes. He is delivered from being stranded.

Let's take the same example again. Only this time he does not discover a boat; he discovers a deserted house and fruit orchard. Inside the house he finds all the tools he will need to cultivate the orchard. Although he is still stranded on the island, he has what he needs to survive. He will be able to carry on.

No doubt we would all agree that the first set of circumstances sounds much better. Yet the man in the second scenario could have been much worse off. In both illustrations the man was provided for; the difference was in the form of the provision.

Oftentimes God demonstrates His faithfulness in adversity by providing for us what we need to survive. He does not change our painful circumstances. He sustains us through them. This is what the writer of Hebrews was referring to when he wrote,

> Let us therefore draw near with confidence to the throne of grace, that we may receive mercy and may find grace to help in time of need.
> —Hebrews 4:16

The writer makes an interesting promise. When we are in need, God will provide us with mercy and grace. This verse does not promise us a change of circumstances, freedom from pain, or deliverance from our enemies. It simply states that when we have a need, God will shower us with mercy and grace. Granted, we would rather have God relieve us of pain than sustain us through it. But He is under no obligation to do so. And He is no less faithful either way.

Paul certainly did not lack confidence in God's faithfulness. Yet God opted not to remove his thorn in the flesh. He chose instead to sustain Paul through it. When Paul asked for relief, the answer he received was simply, "My grace is sufficient for you" (2 Cor. 12:9). In other words, "Paul, you will continue to suffer, but if you hang in there with Me, you will make it."

Grace Beyond Measure

In his fascinating book, *A Shepherd's Look at Psalm 23*, Phillip Keller describes God's wonderful faithfulness during his wife's illness and death. As much as Phillip must have desired to see his wife healed, she was not. Yet he writes,

Again and again I remind myself, "O God, this seems terribly tough, but I know for a fact that in the end it will prove to be the easiest and gentlest way to get me to higher ground." Then when I thank Him for the difficult things, the dark days, I discover that He is there with me in my distress. At that point my panic, my fear, my misgivings give way to calm and quiet confidence in His care. Somehow, in a serene quiet way I am assured all will turn out for my best because He is with me in the valley and things are under His control.

To come to this conviction in the Christian life is to have entered into an attitude of quiet acceptance of every adversity. It is to have moved onto higher ground with God. Knowing Him in this new and intimate manner makes life much more bearable than before.

During my wife's illness and after her death I could not get over the strength, solace and serene outlook imparted to me virtually hour after hour by the presence of God's gracious Spirit Himself. It was as if I was repeatedly refreshed and restored despite the most desperate circumstances all around me.

Could anyone deny God's faithfulness to Phillip? Though God elected not to heal his wife, he was recognizably faithful before, during, and after this painful ordeal. As He did for the apostle Paul, God chose to answer Phillip's cry for help with sustaining grace and mercy.

A Personal Note

I am no different from most people in that I would much rather God deliver me from adversity than sustain me through it. The greatest lessons of my life, however, have been taught to me during times of prolonged adversity. One thing in particular has been a burden on me for twelve years. I have prayed, fasted, and at times literally cried out to God to remove this weight from my shoulders. But His answer every time has been, "Charles, My grace is sufficient for you." And praise God, it is! Every moment of every day it is.

There are times when I operate in my own strength. When I do, I go down under the pressure every time. Then I begin complaining again: "Lord, how do You expect me to be a good husband and father, prepare sermons, and keep everything at church going when I have this extra load to bear as well?" When I finally get quiet enough to listen, He reminds me through His Word or in the privacy of my heart that He does not expect me to do anything on my own. And if I will let Him, He will provide grace and strength in my time of need.

Through all of this I have emerged with a greater sense of who God is. I understand in a much deeper way His commitment to His children. I know beyond a shadow of a doubt that we serve a faithful God, a God who can be trusted in even the darkest valleys, one whose grace is always sufficient and always on time.

Dear friend, I do not know the nature of the adversity you are facing at this time. But I do know that if you will allow Him to, God will use this trial to deepen your faith in His faithfulness. He will reveal Himself to you in ways that are afforded Him only in times of difficulty and heartache.

At no other times are we forced to depend so completely upon the mercy and grace of God. And it is only after we are driven to rely upon His sustaining power that we know it to be adequate; and it is only then that we know in our experience that He is faithful.

Perhaps God has chosen to leave your circumstances the way they are. You may never feel any better. Your spouse may never return. You may never recover financially to the economic level you had previously attained. But God is no less faithful, for He will provide you with mercy and grace in time of need.

The Lord did not say to Paul, "My grace will be sufficient for you," or "My grace has been sufficient for you." He said, "My grace is sufficient." That's in the present tense; that means right now. And so it can be in your experience if you will choose to trust Him. Then you will be able to say with the apostle Paul,

> Most gladly, therefore, I will rather boast about my weaknesses, that the power of Christ may dwell in me.
> —2 Corinthians 12:9

12

Comforted to Comfort

As soon as Bill Jackson entered my office and sat down, I knew he was hurting. Bill was the pastor of a church in another state. He and his family were just finishing their summer vacation and decided at the last minute to swing through Atlanta and visit our church. That last-minute decision proved to be ordered by God.

Bill had been called to River Park Baptist Church about eighteen months prior to his visit with me. During Bill's first year and a half there, God had richly blessed the church. People were being saved, families were being reunited, and there was numerical growth in every area. But some "leaders" were not excited about what was going on. They had been in control for many years, and they felt their control slipping away. Instead of rejoicing over what God was doing, they had begun to speak critically of Bill and his family They said he was neglecting the elderly. They accused him of preaching too many evangelistic sermons. And they did not like his style of leadership—whatever that meant.

As Bill poured out his heart, I had no trouble identifying with everything he was feeling. I had faced a very similar set of circumstances when I came to First Baptist in Atlanta. When he finished, I told him my story. I explained the best I could the hurt I experienced during that time in my life. I described my anger and frustration, my desire to tell the whole crowd what I thought about them. I told him about the times I wanted to walk out.

Then I described for him the amazing ways in which God demonstrated His faithfulness to my family and me. I showed him the passages of Scripture that sustained me. I related the events that finally turned the tide. Then I brought him up to date on all that God has done in our fellowship since then. By the time we were finished, his whole attitude had changed. He was excited about what God was up to at River Park.

As he was leaving, he turned and said, "You know, I really didn't think I would be able to get in to see you. And to be honest, I really didn't think you would be able to understand where I was coming from. Thank God, I was wrong on both counts! I am so encouraged."

That was not the first time I heard a story like Bill's. Neither was it the last. And I have no doubt that God will continue to bring discouraged pastors into my life so that I can share with them and offer encouragement to them. How do I know? Because part of the reason God allowed me to go through that season of adversity was to prepare me for that very thing—to comfort and encourage others who are facing similar circumstances.

God wants each of us involved in the ministry of comforting others. But before you rush to volunteer, keep one thing in mind. It is a very poor comforter who has never needed comforting. So we come to yet another reason God allows adversity to touch our lives: to equip us to comfort others.

Learning the Hard Way

Like so many lessons, I had to learn this one the hard way. For years I had a very simplistic approach to marriage counseling. I believed that if people would just confess their sin, they would live happily ever after. So a couple would come in and tell me their story. I would point out their sin, instruct them to confess it, give them a few verses to memorize, pray with them, and send them on their way. It was a great system because I rarely had to schedule a second appointment. The reason for that, however, was not my tremendous success rate, but people's reluctance to waste any more of their time talking to me.

My problem was that I had never seen a married couple deal with problems from a Christian perspective. My stepfather was not a believer. He and my mother never successfully resolved any of their differences when I was growing up. Up until that point Anna and I had never disagreed about anything major. I really thought that if a couple loved God and kept their sins confessed, everything would be fine. You can imagine what kind of "comforter" I must have been to husbands and wives who were hurting.

196

It is a
very poor
comforter who
has never
needed
comforting.

Then God took advantage of a change in circumstances to increase my sensitivity. In 1970 we moved to Atlanta, and I got too busy. I became married to the ministry and began to neglect my family. It took me several years to see how I was at fault and to put things back in order. Anna experienced a great deal of hurt and rejection during that time. There were moments when I was not sure either of us could go on.

But during that painful process, God made comforters out of each of us because in our low moments He ministered to us in the sweetest ways. Sometimes through understanding friends. Other times through His Word. On many occasions there was just unexplainable peace that permeated my soul. God was our Comforter, our Encourager and, in a literal sense, our Savior.

Today I can feel the hurt of a man or woman who sits in my office and cries. I can identify with the husband who wants desperately to change but is not sure where to begin. I know firsthand the frustration of a woman who loves her husband but feels that her love is not reciprocated. And more important than being able to identify with their hurts, I know how to comfort them, not simply counsel them.

The God of All Comfort

For a long time I believed a person's ability to comfort another was simply a by-product of having experienced suffering. But notice what the apostle Paul says in his letter to the Corinthians:

> Praise be to the God and Father of our Lord Jesus Christ, the Father of compassion and the God of all comfort, who comforts us in all our troubles, so that we can comfort those in any trouble with the comfort we ourselves have received from God. . . . If we are distressed, it is for your comfort and salvation; if we are comforted, it is for your comfort, which produces in you patient endurance of the same sufferings we suffer.
> —2 Corinthians 1:3–4, 6, NIV

According to Paul, God does not comfort the believer for the believer's sake only. Part of His reason for comforting us in our times of distress is so that we can more effectively comfort others. The apostle portrays himself as one who is passing along to other believers the very comfort God used to comfort him.

He goes on, however, to make a strong statement concerning the purpose of suffering in general. He says, "If we are distressed, it is for your comfort." The implication is that part of the purpose for the adversity he was facing was to better enable him to comfort the Corinthian believers. In other words, God sent adversity into his life just to make him a more effective comforter. This was more than a by-product of suffering; it was part of God's purpose.

What was true for the apostle Paul is true for all believers. God allows tragedy to interrupt our lives so that He can comfort us. Once we have dealt with our hurt, He will bring someone across our path with whom we can identify and therefore comfort. As strange and as unnecessary as it may seem on the surface, this is part of God's strategy in maturing us. God is in the business of developing comforters. And the best comforter is one who has struggled with pain or sorrow of some sort and has emerged from that experience victorious through the comfort of another.

Defining Terms

To comfort others is "to impart strength and hope" to them. By strength, I mean Christ's strength. For as I said in a previous chapter, God wants to use adversity to teach us to rely upon Him. The job of a comforter, then, is to move the other persons from relying on their own strength to that of Christ. When we have been used to do that, we have imparted strength.

Every time I read the biography of a great saint I am encouraged by God's grace to that person in times of adversity and difficulty. I come away thinking, If God sustained that individual through such trials, He will sustain me as well. In that way, the testimony imparted strength to me. It motivated me to go on and forget about giving up.

To impart hope is to enable others to take their focus off their immediate circumstances and place it on eternal things. Much of our suffering will not be completely understood or justified in our minds until we see Jesus. In His presence all the loose ends will tie together. All the questions will be answered. The apostle Paul described our hope when he wrote,

Therefore we do not lose heart. Though outwardly we are wasting away, yet inwardly we are being renewed day by day. For our light and momentary troubles are achieving for us an eternal glory that far outweighs them all. So we fix our eyes not on what is seen, but on what is unseen. For what is seen is temporary, but what is unseen is eternal.

—2 Corinthians 4:16–18, NIV

Why did Paul not lose heart when faced with great difficulty? Eternal glory; that which is unseen. Paul's hope was that which is yet to come. That was where he found great comfort. So it is with all of us when the questions raised by adversity run too deep for simple answers. It is not a cop-out to talk about finding answers in heaven. Pointing a person toward eternity is not an act of desperation; it is certainly not a last resort.

In Scripture, the return of the Lord Jesus Christ and His ensuing judgment are almost always presented as encouragements to those undergoing difficulties and trials. In fact, John wrote the entire book of Revelation with that purpose in mind. The Christians of his day were in despair because of the physical persecution they were experiencing from Rome. As the pressure on them continued to mount, the Holy Spirit moved John to write this stirring account of the last days. By his presentation of the fall of Satan and the ultimate and eternal reign of Christ, the believers of his day were encouraged to take heart and endure to the end. John imparted hope to them!

Experience Is Not Enough

Simply experiencing adversity does not automatically prepare a person to comfort others. Only those who have received comfort are capable of giving it. Simply going through hard times is not enough. Comforting someone is more than saying, "I understand" or "The same thing happened to me." Paul said he comforted others with the same comfort he had received from God (see 2 Cor. 1:4). Only persons who have allowed God to comfort them are ready to comfort others.

Your response to adversity will determine whether or not God can use you to comfort others. Many Christians are so thrown off course when adversity strikes that instead of turning to God for comfort, they turn away in anger. When that happens, they miss the purpose for which God allowed adversity to strike in the first place. Not only that, they disqualify themselves as comforters. People who are harboring anger in their hearts cannot truly comfort anyone. As long as their hurt is unresolved, they cannot impart to others the strength of Christ. As long as they are buried under their own circumstances, they cannot offer hope.

The individuals who have allowed (or are allowing) God to walk with them through trials are the ones prepared to comfort others. These people have faced their hurts squarely, drawn on the power of Christ within them, and then put it all in perspective and moved on. These men and women are ready to comfort others.

Allow me to clarify one thing. When I refer to comforters as having dealt with their hurt, I do not mean that they are never bothered by it again. I know people who are forced to deal with certain physical ailments every day of their lives. I am not saying persons in such conditions should come to the point of dealing with their pain once and for all. Neither do I mean that there are no painful memories from past hurts. There are things from my childhood that still bother me to talk about. Both those with continuing adversity as well as those who suffered in the past can be used by God if they have allowed (or are presently allowing) God to comfort and strengthen them.

In Search of Comforters

God is in the process of making you a comforter. He is structuring your experience in such a way as to prepare you for a ministry in someone else's life. As Edith Schaeffer says in *Affliction*:

> No one can really comfort anyone else unless there has been a measure of the same kind of affliction or some kind of suffering which has brought about an understanding and in which we have ourselves experienced the Lord's comfort.

Are you aiding the process by drawing on His divine power? Or are you working against Him by questioning His goodness and love? To resist Him is to miss out not only on the lessons He wants to teach you, but the ministry He is preparing for you in the life of another. It is not a matter of having the right words to say. Neither is it just having experienced the same pain or heartbreak. A comforter is one who has known pain, but along with the pain is the healing, comforting grace of God that ministers strength and hope and encouragement to carry on!

In my book *How to Keep Your Kids on Your Team* I used an illustration that I think bears repeating here. It is a perfect picture of the attitude we are to have toward the adversities we face in light of God's desire to make a comforter of each of us.

A farmer had some puppies he needed to sell. He painted a sign advertising the pups and set about nailing it to a post on the edge of his yard. As he was driving the last nail into the post, he felt a tug on his overalls. He looked down into the eyes of a little boy.

"Mister," he said, "I want to buy one of your puppies."

"Well," said the farmer, as he rubbed the sweat off the back of his neck, "these puppies come from fine parents and cost a good deal of money."

The boy dropped his head for a moment. Then reaching deep into his pocket, he pulled out a handful of change and held it up to the farmer. "I've got thirty-nine cents. Is that enough to take a look?"

"Sure," said the farmer. And with that he let out a whistle. "Here, Dolly!" he called. Out from the doghouse and down the ramp ran Dolly followed by four little balls of fur. The little boy pressed his face against the chain link fence. His eyes danced with delight.

As the dogs made their way to the fence, the little boy noticed something else stirring inside the doghouse. Slowly another little ball appeared; this one noticeably smaller. Down the ramp it slid. Then in a somewhat awkward manner the little pup began hobbling toward the others, doing its best to catch up. This was clearly the runt of the litter.

"I want that one," the little boy said, pointing to the runt.

The farmer knelt down at the boy's side and said, "Son, you don't want that puppy. He will never be able to run and play with you like these other dogs would."

With that the little boy stepped back from the fence, reached down, and began rolling up one leg of his trousers. In doing so he revealed a steel brace running down both sides of his leg attaching itself to a specially made shoe. Looking back up at the farmer, he said, "You see, sir, I don't run too well myself, and he will need someone who understands."

My friend, the world is full of people who need someone who understands. That is the ministry to which God has called each of us.

13

Not I, But Christ

When our kids were in elementary school, Anna and I decided it was time to begin teaching them to make decisions for themselves. We began with small things, such as what to wear, where the family should eat, and where we should go for vacation. Every once in a while, however, our system hit a snag. Like most youngsters, our kids had an unquenchable desire to please Mom and Dad—that is, most of the time. Consequently, there would be times when we would leave a decision in their hands, and their response would be, "What do you want us to do?" Our natural tendency was to tell them. But we realized that to do so would simply interfere with the development of their decision-making skills. We tried to stay involved with the decision-making process, but we allowed them to make the final decision.

Oftentimes this created a frustrating situation for the kids. "Why won't you just tell me what you want me to do?" one of them would ask. "We want you to learn to make decisions on your own," we would reply. "I don't want to make decisions. I want to do what you want me to do," our child would answer.

As I think back on those somewhat comical exchanges, I am reminded of our relationship with the heavenly Father. The reason we and the children went round and round about the simplest issues is the same reason we are confused by much of what our heavenly Father allows. We had different goals. Anna and I were trying to prepare our kids for life. They just wanted direction. To have always given them answers would have made it easier on them in the short run, but it would have handicapped them later. There was bound to be conflict either way. If, however, the children would have understood then how important it was to learn to make decisions, and if somehow, as youngsters, they could have developed the same perspective and goals that Anna and I shared, things would have been easier all the way around.

Our goals and perspective on life determine our response to adversity. If your ultimate aim in life in any way conflicts with that of our heavenly Father, confusion is inevitable. Somewhere down the line He will structure your experience in such a way that it appears as if He is working against you rather than for you. Your natural reaction will be to wonder if He is paying attention, if maybe He has forgotten about you. But in reality He is just involved in the next stage of your development. What is progress to Him will likely have every appearance of abandonment to you.

This past week I was talking to a woman in our fellowship who is undergoing chemotherapy. As a result she has lost all of her hair. Following each treatment, she spends fifteen to sixteen hours throwing up. She has no energy. Every area of her life has been affected. Her response?

> Pastor, I thought for sure I would be able to minister to patients in the waiting room. But I realize now that it is my nurse who God wants to speak to. She cannot figure out how my hus-

Our goals
and perspective
on life determine
our response
to adversity.

band and I have such a good attitude about this whole thing. We had a wonderful opportunity to explain how God uses those in the medical profession as His tools while He does the actual healing.

I stood there in amazement. No bitterness. No doubts. Just pure, childlike faith that God was still in control. Her perspective was right in line with her heavenly Father's. She was looking for the good He would no doubt bring about through this whole ordeal. She did not deny the pain and the occasional fear she experienced. But she refused to allow her thoughts to remain there. Instead she was looking for God's hand at work in the midst of her adversity, just as she had always looked for His hand during times of health and prosperity. Again, your goals and perspective on life will determine your response to adversity.

What's the Point?

As I have stated earlier, God's goal for you and me is not ease, comfort, or pleasure. Neither is it that we simply avoid eternal condemnation. Many Christians believe, however, that these two ideas are the sum total of God's will for their lives. Listen to their prayers. They are filled with references to health, protection, guidance, and safety. Then to top it off they pray, "Lord, please be with us as we go." What do they think He is going to do? Wait there until they come back? Again, the implication is, "Lord, we know Your number one concern is our safety, health, and protection. Go with us now and keep us safe."

In the last few chapters I have discussed several reasons God allows adversity. Each of these can be thought of as a spoke in a wheel. In this chapter I want to concentrate on the hub. What is God really trying to accomplish in all of this? Why deal with our pride and independence? Why discipline us? Why make us better comforters? The answer goes back once again to God's goal for His children. The apostle Paul described that goal this way:

> Blessed be the God and Father of our Lord Jesus Christ, who has blessed us with every spiritual blessing in the heavenly places in Christ, just as He chose us in Him before the founda- tion of the world, **that we should be**

holy and blameless before Him.
—Ephesians 1:3–4 (emphasis mine)

What is His goal for us? That we should be "holy" and "blameless." Paul made a similar statement in Colossians:

And although you were formerly alienated and hostile in mind, engaged in evil deeds, yet He has now reconciled you in His fleshly body through death, **in order to present you before Him holy and blameless and beyond reproach**—if indeed you continue in the faith firmly established and steadfast.
—Colossians 1:21–23 (emphasis mine)

And again in Romans:

For whom He foreknew, He also predestined to become **conformed to the image of His Son**, that He might be the first-born among many brethren.
—Romans 8:29(emphasis mine)

God's ultimate goal for us is that we be conformed to the "image" of His Son—in other words, Christlikeness. This is what we were made for. But what does that mean? I have heard it said that Christlikeness is simply doing what Christ would do in every situation. Along the same line, some say it is a matter of imitating Christ. I believe there is a place for this kind of thinking and application in the Christian life. But what Paul is referring to goes much deeper than that. A lost person could imitate Christ. Many good and moral men and women have lived lives that put many Christians to shame, and yet they never put their faith in Christ. Certainly they were not holy and blameless before God. What, then, is Paul referring to?

Imitation Versus Impartation

God's goal for us is not that we merely imitate the life of Christ. His desire is that the life of Christ be lived through us. The difference is this: we can do many good, Christlike things and still be controlled by "self." Think about our motives sometimes for the "Christlike" things we do. We pray when we have a need. We read the Bible for comfort or direction. We are kind to people so they will be kind in return. We give because the preacher asks us to. We witness only when highly motivated. We attend church out of habit. Does that sound like Christ? Yet all those activities are things He did on earth. Something is wrong.

The problem is that we can be totally controlled by "self" and yet be busy about the "Lord's work." We rarely take time to look beneath the surface and examine why we do what we do and in whose strength we operate. Think about your prayers. Who do they center on? Oftentimes it is "self." God becomes a means to an end. Instead of getting involved with God's agenda, we spend our energy trying to get Him involved with what is significant to us: prosperity, peace, acceptance, and so on. As a result we become very religious but not very Christlike.

Remember how Christ prayed? "Thy will be done, on earth as it is in heaven." When is the last time you prayed an open-ended prayer like that? "Lord, whatever You want to do, do it. However You want to use me, use me. Whatever You want to accomplish through me, Thy will be done!" "Self" does not like prayers like that. There is too much to lose, too much sacrifice involved. "Self" always has an agenda that benefits itself.

Christ's agenda was to please the Father

and accomplish His will at any cost. On the eve of His death we find Him saying,

My Father, if it is possible, let this cup pass from Me; yet not as I will, but as Thou wilt.　　　—Matthew 26:39

That is the attitude God wants to develop in each of His children. Total surrender to the unannounced will of God. An attitude that says, "Yes, yes, yes. Now, what is it You want me to do?" Christlikeness is not "self" camouflaged in Christlike activities. It is an attitude that flows from the very life of Christ Himself as He indwells the believer.

Adversity?

At this point you are probably wondering what all this has to do with adversity. God is not satisfied with well-mannered, respectable "self" on the throne of our lives. He wants to remove all traces of "self" so that we can be presented to Christ holy and blameless. One way God accomplishes that is by sending adversity into our lives. Adversity stirs us up and causes us to look at life differently. We are forced to deal with things on a deeper level. Nothing causes "self" to cave in like suffering. And once our religious facade begins to wear thin, God moves in and begins teaching us what real Christlikeness is all about.

"Self's" first reaction to adversity is to begin looking for sin to confess. But it is not because "self" is concerned with holiness. "Self" is concerned with preservation. And if confessing sin will influence God to turn off the heat, then so be it. When that does not work, "self" becomes desperate. Oftentimes "self" will then bury itself in religious service, saying, "Certainly God would not allow a diligent servant like me to suffer." But God just turns up the heat.

Death to Self

God's goal for "self" is clearly outlined in Scripture. The apostle Paul summed it up this way:

> I have been crucified with Christ; and it is no longer I who live, but Christ lives in me; and the life which I now live in the flesh I live by faith in the Son of God, who loved me, and delivered Himself up for me.
> —Galatians 2:20

God wants the "self" life crucified. He does not want it dressed up, patched up, under control, decorated, or ordained. He wants it crucified. Paul said that there was a sense in which he was crucified with Christ. And the life he lived was no longer his life. That is, the life expressed through him was not "self" trying to imitate Christ. He said Christ was living through him. The actual life of Jesus Christ was being expressed through his body, through his flesh and blood. He describes the same experience a little differently in Romans:

> Or do you not know that all of us who have been baptized into Christ Jesus have been baptized into His death? Therefore we have been buried with Him through baptism into death, in order that as Christ was raised from the dead through the glory of the Father, so we too might walk in newness of life. . . . knowing this, that our old self was crucified with Him, that our body of sin might be done away with, that we should no longer be slaves to sin; for he who has died is freed from sin.
>
> —Romans 6:3–4, 6–7

Paul says our "old self" was crucified with Him. As a result we now have the privilege of walking in "newness of life." Whose life? Christ's life. Christlikeness is not simply the imitation of a life. It is the impartation of new life—His life!

This is the experience into which God wants to bring all of His children: personal identification with Christ, specifically, the death and resurrection of Christ. Ultimately, this is accomplished on a daily basis through faith. Believers go about their daily responsibilities trusting Christ to express Himself through their individual personalities.

Back to the Drawing Board

Many believers are ignorant of this doctrine. Once they trust Christ as their Savior, they immediately try to Christianize "self." Consequently, many well-meaning Christians spend years trying to make "self" look and act like Christ. Layers and layers of good works are piled on. Hours and hours of prayer are added. All of this is fortified by sermons and seminars and tapes and books, and on and on it goes.

In many respects they are actually hindering the will of God in their lives. Sooner or later, because of His unwavering commitment to finish what He has begun, God begins to peel away the layers of "self." This is usually a painful process because it involves exposing the inadequacy of "self." That means failure at those things that were once considered one's forte.

Oftentimes this process involves a stripping away of self-confidence. Sometimes God moves in on "self" through a person's finances. Other times it is through health. Everybody is different. And everybody's "self" life has its own makeup. But God knows just how to peel away the layers so as to force His children to deal with their Christian life on a completely different level. "Self" always has an Achilles' heel. And God knows just where it is.

Losing to Win

Through the years, I have watched God perform some radical "self" removals on folks. Although their circumstances differ, the pattern is somewhat the same. God is in the process of breaking a man on our maintenance staff even now. When I first met Phillip, he was a few days away from becoming one of Atlanta's many street people.

He had come to the end of his financial resources, and he had nowhere to go but the streets. At one time he had been a successful businessman. Slowly his luck turned sour. First, he lost his business. To make ends meet, he went to work for a company doing the same type of work at which he had been successful for years. He failed miserably and was laid off. As a result of his financial situation, his wife left him and went to live in another state. Phillip turned in his company car, packed up his few belongings, and hitchhiked to Atlanta. To this day, he is not sure why he chose our city.

We found Phillip a place to live and gave him a job. After talking with him a few times, I realized he was dealing with deep depression over all that had transpired. I also recognized God's hand at work in Phillip's life. God was marching "self" to the cross. Every time I passed Phillip in the hall I would ask him how it was going. For the first couple of months he would hang his head and tell me how lonely and angry and frustrated he was. "I don't know how much more I can take. It seems I can't do anything right. Nothing is working out. I used to be responsible for buildings twice this size. And here I am back doing the kind of work I was doing ten years ago."

In the months that followed, God began to transform Phillip. Through counseling, he began to understand what it meant to be identified with the death of Christ. It began to get through to him that he had been given new life. For a while when I would check on him, he would smile and say, "I don't understand all of this yet, but by faith, Christ is my life."

Then I got news that Phillip's wife had called and said she was never coming back. I knew this would devastate him. We had been praying that God would soften her heart and restore their marriage. Now it looked as if there was no hope.

I found Phillip busy at work by the kitchen. I put my arm around him ready to provide the comfort I imagined he would need. But the look on his face told me a different story. "I understand now," he said. "Christ is my life. I still don't understand it all, but praise God, I don't have to understand it to experience it." I asked him how he was doing in view of his last conversation with his wife. "Great," he said. "I don't know why, but I am doing great. It is all in the hands of the Lord now, and He is my life."

Only the Lord knows what is going to

happen with Phillip's marriage. His wife has not changed her position. But Phillip is going to make it. In our last conversation Phillip admitted that he would never have come to understand his identification with Christ apart from losing everything else he was dependent upon.

The Way of the Cross

"So," you ask, "can people come to the cross without having their whole lives ripped apart?" Absolutely. The path to the cross is not the same for everybody. It is far easier for some than others. The thing to remember is that marching "self" to the cross is God's number one goal insofar as a person's sanctification is concerned. Once He begins, He will not let up until "self" is dethroned and crucified. Then, and only then, will you be free to experience the very life of Christ flowing through your personality. Your whole Christian experience will be radically different. God will no longer be a means to an end; He will be the end. To know Him will be enough.

The idea of total surrender will no longer leave you paralyzed with fear. On the contrary, it will become the most exciting chal-

225

lenge in life. Every day will bring with it new opportunities for the very life of the Savior to be poured out through you. "Newness of life" will no longer be a theological concept; it will be your experience. Christianity was never meant to be a form of self-improvement. God is not interested in improving "self"; His concern is with crucifying it.

Dear friend, is God marching you to the cross? If so, is He having to drag you kicking and screaming, or are you going willingly? Refusing to surrender only prolongs the pain. Remember, the One who has engineered what may appear to be unbearable conditions is the same One who gave His only begotten Son to die for your sins. As much as it may seem that He has turned against you, that is not the case. The situation can be compared to that of an earthly father who has set about to remove slivers of glass from his child's foot. To run would be to inflame the wound. To cry out in protest only delays the inevitable.

In his classic work *Mere Christianity*, C. S. Lewis has this to say about Christ and the "self" life:

The terrible thing, the almost impossible thing, is to hand over your whole self—all your wishes and precautions—to Christ. But it is far easier than what we are all trying to do instead. For what we are trying to do is to remain what we call "ourselves" to keep personal happiness as our great aim in life, and yet at the same time be "good." We are all trying to let our mind and heart go their own way—centered on money or pleasure or ambition—and hoping, in spite of this, to behave honestly and chastely and humbly. And that is exactly what Christ warned us you could not do. As He said, a thistle cannot produce figs. If I am a field that contains nothing but grass-seed, I cannot produce wheat. Cutting the grass may keep it short: but I shall still produce grass and no wheat. If I want to produce wheat, the change must go deeper than the surface. I must be ploughed up and re-sown.

Is God in the process of plowing you up? If He is, don't resist. Your heavenly Father loves you too much and has paid too high a price to let you go your own way. He wants you to come to the end of yourself. He wants you to admit defeat. He wants you to entrust your life, your future, your possessions, your relationships, your all to Him. And then just when you think all is lost, He wants to replace what He has taken, not with things, but with Himself. C. S. Lewis interpreted God's intent in this way:

> Hand over the whole natural self, all the desires which you think innocent as well as the ones you think wicked— the whole outfit. I will give you a new self instead. In fact, I will give you Myself.

Amen!

14

One Man's Story

I am usually leery of autobiographies. It is next to impossible to interpret one's own experience with much objectivity. An individual's story as described by someone who knew the person usually offers a more realistic picture. On the other hand, once I have been exposed to and encouraged by the experience of another as portrayed in a biography, I oftentimes wish for a personal interview, an opportunity to know firsthand what drove that person and what thoughts occurred during challenging circumstances and how successes and failures were handled.

After reading the biography of C. T. Studd, I had a burning desire to know how he dealt with the loneliness of being separated from his wife all those many years while serving God on separate continents. I think about Jim Elliot and the courage he displayed as he confronted the Auca Indians. What was running through his mind in the moments just preceding his death at the hands of those whom he had come to serve?

The ideal situation would be to have a biography written by an objective observer along with an autobiographical commentary of what the character was feeling and thinking in the events of life. With two accounts we would have a trustworthy historical sketch as well as personal insight into the man or woman.

An Ideal Situation

God has been gracious enough to provide us with just such an ideal account. In the book of Acts, Luke gives us a running narrative of Paul's trials and tribulations. Luke was a companion of the apostle Paul. Throughout the book he refers to "we" and "us" when speaking of the events Paul encountered (see Acts 16:10–17; 20:5–21; 27:1–28:16). Luke accompanied Paul to Macedonia. He headed up the work in Phillippi. Eventually he ended up with Paul in Rome during the apostle's house arrest. It was probably during this period that he wrote the book of Acts.

When Paul talks about affliction and trials and persecutions, it is not just his word that we have to go on. Luke was an eyewitness to much of what Paul claims to have experienced and there would be no reason for him to lie. Luke was motivated to record these things so that there would be an accurate historical record (see Luke 1:1–4). In light of all this, we can have confidence that the suffering Paul claims to have experienced was real.

But that is only half the good news. Not only has God provided us with an eyewitness account of Paul's trials, He has allowed us to possess Paul's own commentary of these same events. We don't have to wonder why Paul endured. We are not left to speculate as to how he remained faithful through his various trials. Neither are we forced to depend totally on someone else's interpretation of Paul's inner battles with pain and suffering. We have his personal testimony.

We should take advantage of this unique combination of documents in our possession and dig out every nugget of truth concerning adversity. In Paul, we have a man who suffered extensively on every level, and yet remained faithful to the end—something that cannot yet be said of you or me.

What did Paul have to say about adversity? What did he learn? What was his secret? How did he keep picking himself up over and over again when most men would have quit? The answer to almost all these questions can be found in one section of Paul's second letter to the church in Corinth:

> And because of the surpassing greatness of the revelations, for this reason, to keep me from exalting myself, there was given me a thorn in the flesh, a messenger of Satan to buffet me— to keep me from exalting myself! Concerning this I entreated the Lord three times that it might depart from me. And He has said to me, "My grace is sufficient for you, for power is perfected in weakness." Most gladly, therefore, I will rather boast about my weaknesses, that the power of Christ may dwell in me. Therefore I am well content with weaknesses, with insults, with distresses, with persecutions,

with difficulties, for Christ's sake; for when I am weak, then I am strong.
     —2 Corinthians 12:7–10

Of all the hardships and abuse Paul suffered, his "thorn in the flesh" bothered him most. As stated earlier, no one is sure what Paul is referring to here. Some have said it was his wife. Others say it was sexual temptation. I believe it was a physical problem of some sort.

The term itself is used in literature of the same period to refer to a splinter. When used figuratively, this word refers to anything that is a constant annoyance. In the context of Paul's discussion, this may be somewhat of an understatement. Although his thorn was constant, it was more than just a little annoying. Paul's thorn was a source of great concern.

Paul's Discoveries

As we have observed in previous chapters, God chose not to remove this thorn, and Paul learned to live with it. In the process, however, Paul made some fantastic discoveries about adversity that enabled him not to merely survive his circumstances, but to "glory" in them and emerge victorious. So what did Paul discover?

I. There Is a Divine Purpose Behind All Adversity.

> And **because** of the surpassing greatness of the revelations, **for this reason**, to keep me from exalting myself, there was given me a thorn in the flesh.
> —2 Corinthians 12:7 (emphasis mine)

Paul understood that God was always using adversity to further His cause; it always had a purpose. In the preceding chapters we examined in detail several of God's purposes in allowing adversity to touch our lives. Unfortunately, they are not always easily identified, and there is oftentimes a gap between our experience and our understanding. We can go for days, weeks, years, and sometimes a lifetime without knowing God's purpose.

Job went to his grave without ever knowing why he suffered. Paul says he entreated the Lord three times before receiving an answer. The way the verse reads, it sounds as if Paul asked God once in the morning, once after lunch, and then one more time in the evening. But we do not know how much time elapsed between his petitions. Like us, Paul knew the frustration of trying to maintain faith in God while at the same time wondering why He did not respond.

What Paul learned, and what we must learn as well, is that when God does not remove our "thorn," it is not without reason. God would not have us suffer for the sake of suffering. There is always a purpose.

2. God May Choose to Reveal the Purpose for Our Adversity.

In Paul's case, God chose to indicate why he was given the "thorn." It was to keep him from becoming proud. It is interesting that God did not reveal this to Paul the first time he prayed. There is a reason for that. Notice that Paul prayed, "Concerning this I entreated the Lord three times that it might depart from me." Paul did not even ask God why. He was asking that it be removed.

It is not uncommon for God to reveal the reason for suffering. He revealed to Moses the reason he was not allowed to enter the Promised Land. God told Joshua why he and his army were defeated at Ai. Jesus told the disciples that they could expect trouble and why. John wrote to the churches of his day and explained why they were experiencing trials. And James used the first part of his epistle to explain why the believers of his day were suffering. God is not necessarily silent concerning the question of why. But He answers according to His schedule, which is usually slightly behind ours.

3. God Never Scolds Us for Asking Why or for Requesting That the Adversity Be Removed.

There is no evidence that God scolded Paul for asking that his thorn be removed. God understands our weakness. He expects us to cry out to Him when we are experiencing hurt or frustration. He desires that we cast our cares on Him. Why? Because in doing so we are expressing faith, and faith is the foundation of our entire relationship with Him.

Paul was not the first to cry out to God for help. His own Son found Himself facing pain and rejection of the worst kind. In His own way, He, too, asked that a thorn be removed—the cross.

> And He went a little beyond them, and fell on His face and prayed, saying, "My Father, if it is possible, let this cup pass from Me."
> —Matthew 26:39

You need not feel guilty for asking God to remove adversity from your life. He expects it. At the same time, as we have seen, your prayer may not be answered in the fashion or moment you would prefer. But nevertheless, you should ask, for it was during the process of asking for relief that Paul received a word from God.

In the same way, we should not be afraid to ask God why, either. So often I hear people say, "I am not asking God why He allowed this; I am just trusting that He is in control." I understand the motivation behind such a statement. It is meant as an expression of faith and trust in the sovereignty and presence of God. And I would never fault individuals for their faith. But nowhere in Scripture are we admonished to refrain from asking why. As we have already seen, there are plenty of examples in Scripture where God was more than willing to answer that question.

James actually instructs believers to ask God for an answer to the "why" question. After encouraging his readers to focus on how God is using adversity in their lives, he says,

> But if any of you lacks wisdom, let him ask of God, who gives to all men generously and without reproach, and it will be given to him.
>
> —James 1:5

In effect, he is saying, "If in the middle of all these trials you have any questions, go ahead and ask God." Then notice the second half: "Who gives to all men generously and without reproach." God is a generous God. Not only that, He is not going to get upset if we question Him as to what is happening.

The question of why becomes a problem when it is asked in doubt. That is, we assume that because *we* see no purpose in suffering, there is none. To the one who asks why from that point of reference, James says,

> Let not that man expect that he will receive anything from the Lord, being a double-minded man, unstable in all his ways.   —James 1:7–8

Just as an earthly father desires to comfort his children in times of distress, so our heavenly Father desires to comfort us. And when in His wisdom He believes the answer to the question of why is important for us to know, He will reveal it.

4. Adversity May Be a Gift from God.

When we think of adversity, we are oftentimes prone to think of it as something God does to us. Our prayers reflect that attitude: "Lord, why did this happen to me?" "Father, why are You allowing this to happen to me?" Prayers such as these reflect our basic heartfelt conviction—adversity at best is bad! And so it is viewed as something that happens to us.

Paul did not view it that way at all. Notice his phraseology when referring to his thorn in the flesh:

> For this reason, to keep me from exalting myself, there was **given** me a thorn in the flesh.
> —2 Corinthians 12:7 (emphasis mine)

Paul had the faith to believe that this constant irritation was a gift. As godly a fellow

239

as the apostle Paul may have been, I doubt that his attitude started out this positive. But as he grew to understand what God was doing in his life, his attitude began to change. And in the process he saw his thorn for what it was—a gift.

It was a gift in that it was through this irritation that God protected Paul from the thing he feared the most—spiritual disqualification (see 1 Cor. 9:27). Paul had a burning desire to end well, to finish the course God had set before him. He knew from watching others that nothing destroys a man's or woman's effectiveness for God as quickly and as thoroughly as pride. Therefore, if his thorn in the flesh would protect him from pride, it was indeed a gift from God. He could with all sincerity view it as something God did for him rather than to him.

5. Satan Can Be the Agent of Adversity.

Things certainly become confusing at this point. Paul just finished saying that God was the One who arranged for him to live with this thorn in the flesh. Then he explained that it was really a gift in light of its intended result. Just as things were making good sense, he stated,

> There was given me a thorn in the flesh, **a messenger of Satan** to buffet me.
> —2 Corinthians 12:7 (emphasis mine)

Now wait, is God behind this, or Satan? How is it that a messenger of Satan is now working for the good of one of God's servants? That seems like a total contradiction. Everybody has an opinion at this point. But we stay on solid theological ground if we take the text at face value. And the implication is that God uses messengers of Satan in the lives of His servants. What more can we say?

Actually, this point should be very comforting. When we take what is stated here and compare it to the life of Job, we gain a clearer picture of God's sovereignty. Even the schemes of the devil can be used to benefit us and further the kingdom of God. Think about it. Even Satan's host works under the watchful eye of our Father in heaven.

6. God Will Comfort Us in Our Adversities.

The answer Paul received from God concerning his thorn in the flesh was not what he expected. We know from his prayer that it was not what he really wanted, either. Yet

Paul was able to take great comfort in the fact that he received an answer. God's response to Paul served to assure him that he had not been abandoned. He was not suffering alone. God was still in control and still at work in Paul's life.

Our Lord has promised never to leave or forsake us. He made this promise at a time when those who had followed Him faithfully were about to launch out into a work that would be difficult. God demonstrated His faithfulness to those men, and He will do the same in your life and my life.

The primary reason we are not aware of God's comfort during times of adversity is that we don't look for it. We give up. We begin to doubt His wisdom, His goodness, and at times His very existence. Doubt diminishes our ability to recognize the comforting hand of God. It clouds our spiritual vision. Once we doubt God's goodness and faithfulness, we will miss His efforts to comfort us.

7. God's Grace Is Sufficient During Times of Adversity.

God did not give Paul what he requested. But what He gave him was far better in the long run. God granted Paul the grace he needed to bear up under the pressure brought about by his thorn in the flesh. To say that Paul was able merely to bear up under the pressure is to understate the case, however. Paul endured his hardship victoriously! Notice how he describes his situation:

> And He has said to me, "My grace is sufficient for you, for power is perfected in weakness." Most gladly, therefore, I will rather boast about my weaknesses, that the power of Christ may dwell in me.
> —2 Corinthians 12:9

This does not sound like a man who is just barely getting by. We don't find Paul dwelling on his hardships and his trials in a depressing manner. Rather, we find him rejoicing over weaknesses. He is not excited about the weaknesses themselves; he is exultant over the fact that God's grace empowers him to reign victoriously over his weaknesses.

Paul discovered what many believers miss throughout their whole lives. That is, God's power is most evident to us when we are weak. It is most evident then to others as well. Paul understood he was far more effective when forced through weakness to rely on God's power through him, and so he says he gladly boasts about his weaknesses.

Paul's testimony is an encouragement to me in this one area more than any other. If God's grace was sufficient for a man who left his family, his home, and his friends to plant churches in hostile environments; who was shipwrecked, imprisoned, stoned, and left for dead; I am confident His grace is more than sufficient for anything I will encounter.

8. God May Not See Fit to Remove the Adversity.

This is the most difficult principle of all to accept—not only in the context of our own lives, but in the lives of those we love as well. How many times have you seen someone suffering and thought, Lord, why don't You do something? There is a woman in our fellowship who has calcium deposits all along her spinal column. Her back is bent over so far that she is unable to look up. Every Sunday one of our faithful men and his daughter bring her to church. As they lead her down the aisle to her regular pew, I always think,

Lord, how great it would be if You would heal that dear saint. And yet it seems that this is an adversity He has chosen not to remove.

Many Christians have the idea that if they pray enough and believe enough, they can force God's hand; they think He will be compelled to remove their adversity. They misuse Scripture to build a case for the divine healing of every disease and affliction. The Scriptures, however, make no such claim. I certainly believe in divine healing. In fact, all healing is divine. But nowhere in the Bible are we promised exemption from disease and illness in this life. This world is still under a curse. And these dying and decaying bodies of ours are cursed right along with everything else.

I think about Joni Eareckson Tada, who is a beautiful testimony of God's grace in a life. She does not suffer from a lack of faith. It takes far more faith to endure confinement to a wheelchair than it does to believe Jesus can heal. Joni realizes that Jesus could heal her in a moment. But she has realized that for the time being He has chosen to use her as she is.

Jesus never promised to remove our pain and suffering in this life. Certainly there are cases in which He does. Some are quite miraculous. But these are the exceptions, not the rule. Jesus told His disciples,

> In the world you have tribulation, but take courage; I have overcome the world. —John 16:33

Paul knew what it meant to live with adversity. He knew the frustration of realizing that relief would never come; having asked three times, he was denied. Yet he did not complain and grow bitter; he did not doubt the goodness and mercy of God. He experienced instead the power of God. Paul learned to depend daily on God's grace. He was even able to accept the fact that God would be doing him a disservice by removing his thorn in the flesh. And so he learned to be content, even in the midst of constant suffering.

No one likes to suffer. In our hearts, we all desire immediate relief from pain and grief. God understands our weakness and our sorrow. There are times, however, when despite our inconvenience, He allows adversity to persist. The best thing we can do is simply submit to His sovereign decision, knowing that His grace will be sufficient for anything we might face.

9. Contentment Does Not Hinge on the Nature of Our Circumstances.

I have met many discontented people in my life. Always on the move. Forever arranging and rearranging their lives. Never satisfied with themselves or their circumstances. The underlying premise from which most of their decisions flow is that personal contentment is inextricably linked to one's circumstances. In other words, a person's surroundings—job, spouse, income, residence—determine peace of mind and satisfaction. Consequently, when they become dissatisfied with life, they begin changing things. They quit their job. They sell their house. They trade their car. Or in some cases, they look for a new marriage partner. Soon, however, that same feeling begins gnawing at them again. And off they go, making more changes.

Now if you will think about it, nobody needed a change of scenery more than the apostle Paul. His life seemed to go from bad to worse. In this same letter he lists the perils he faced in attempting to spread the gospel:

> Five times I received from the Jews
> thirty-nine lashes. Three times I was

beaten with rods, once I was stoned, three times I was shipwrecked, a night and a day I have spent in the deep. I have been on frequent journeys, in dangers from rivers, dangers from robbers, dangers from my countrymen, dangers from the Gentiles, dangers in the city, dangers in the wilderness, dangers on the sea, dangers among false brethren; I have been in labor and hardship through many sleepless nights, in hunger and thirst, often without food, in cold and exposure.

—2 Corinthians 11:24–27

Having experienced all of that, he is still able to say,

Therefore I am well content with weaknesses, with insults, with distresses, with persecutions, with difficulties, for Christ's sake; for when I am weak, then I am strong.

—2 Corinthians 12:10

He echoes the same idea in his letter to the Philippian believers:

Not that I speak from want; for I have learned to be content in whatever circumstances I am. I know how to get along with humble means, and I also know how to live in prosperity; in any and every circumstance I have learned the secret of being filled and going hungry, both of having abundance and suffering need.

—Philippians 4:11–12

If Paul was able to find contentment in the midst of those hostile environments, I think it is safe to say that contentment does not hinge on one's circumstances. Paul faced adversity at every level—everything from prison to sickness to rejection by his own people. Yet he claimed to be "well content."

Paul's "secret," as he referred to it in Philippians, was his relationship with Christ. He discovered that true and lasting contentment is found not in things, but in a Person. He could be content in the most adverse circumstances because his aim in life was to be pleasing to the Lord (see 2 Cor. 5:9). Knowing that he was where his Lord wanted him to be was enough. He did not need material props to bring him satisfaction.

You may say, "Well, that sounds mighty spiritual, but how realistic is it to think that we can find contentment outside the realm of our circumstances?" I believe it is extremely realistic. And I don't believe this is a principle that applies to some elite group of believers. This kind of contentment is for all Christians. Otherwise we will spend the bulk of our time and energy trying to better our circumstances rather than serving Christ. I am not against self-improvement. But I have a real problem with believers who are so caught up in upgrading their lifestyle that they have little time for God and His church.

For Paul, learning to be content in every circumstance was a necessity. He would not have survived if this principle did not work. Yet as we have seen, Paul did more than simply survive; he "reigned" in life through Christ (see Rom. 5:17). Contentment is available to all of us, regardless of our circumstances, if we will only commit our lives to the purposes and plan of God.

10. The Key to Advancing Through Adversity Is to View It as for Christ's Sake.

Paul understood that his purpose in life was to bring glory to God by preaching the gospel of Christ. Therefore, anything that happened to him in the process of obeying God was really for Christ's sake. That is, people were not rejecting him. They were rejecting his message and thus Christ.

> Therefore I am well content with weaknesses, with insults, with distresses, with persecutions, with difficulties, **for Christ's sake**; for when I am weak, then I am strong.
> —2 Corinthians 12:10 (emphasis mine)

Paul did not take personally what was happening to him. He realized that his suffering was the direct result of his mission in life. Even his thorn in the flesh was for Christ's sake, to keep him from forfeiting his ministry and damaging the cause of Christ. Paul was not glorying in suffering for suffering's sake. It was for Christ's sake. There was purpose in all he experienced.

Your mission in life is to bring glory to God by spreading the gospel of Christ. You may never stand in a pulpit. You may never leave your hometown. Regardless of where you go or the opportunities you have, your mission is still the same. When you become consumed by God's call on your life, everything will take on new meaning and significance. You will begin to see every facet of your life—including your pain—as a means through which God can work to bring others to Himself. When God uses the adversity in your life to draw people to Himself, you have suffered for Christ's sake.

We know God can use our time, our money, and our talent. Why not our suffering? I have heard many invitations in which preachers have asked people to dedicate children, homes, and businesses to the Lord's service. I have yet to hear a preacher challenge his people to dedicate their adversity to the Lord. Yet nothing gets the attention of the lost world more quickly than a saint who is suffering successfully. Sorrow and grief are powerful tools in the right hands.

For whose sake are you suffering? Most people suffer for their own sake. Consequently, they become bitter, angry, and difficult to live with. Paul realized his suffering was for Christ's sake. It was just one more means of expressing the glory and grace of God to a lost world. God may want to relieve you of the adversity in your life. But He may choose to delay your deliverance that He might use your suffering for His sake. Cruel, you ask? It may seem so now. But remember that He spared not His own Son. You and I have eternal life today because Christ suffered and died for His Father's sake. It was through the Lord's pain that many were reconciled to God. And we who say we know Him ought to walk even as He walked. That is, we should make our pain available to God for Him to use as He desires. And then we, too, will endure these things for Christ's sake.

Looking Back

As I think back over these ten lessons Paul learned about adversity, he almost appears larger than life. He makes it sound so simple. It appears that way because by the time Paul penned this letter to the church in Corinth he had assimilated these principles into his lifestyle. It is just like watching players in a professional tennis match. They make it look so simple. I find myself wanting to go home, get out my racket, and start smashing tennis balls as hard as I can. Because it looks as if that is all they are doing. What I don't see are the hours and hours of practice and evaluation they go through before they ever get to the match.

As we read the life of Paul, in Acts and in his various epistles, we are seeing him at his best, at the end of a lifetime of learning. That is not to take away from what he says. On the contrary, what we read in 2 Corinthians 12 should be very encouraging. It sets before us what is possible if we press on. It serves as a constant reminder of God's abiding grace. It stands as a warning to those who would shake their fist at God when adversity strikes. Paul's life was filled with such extreme suffering that each of us must think, If God could sustain him through that, I don't have anything to worry about.

You really don't have anything to worry about. God's grace is, even now as you are reading, sufficient for whatever you are facing. Your responsibility is to submit yourself to the lordship of Christ and say,

> Have Thine own way, Lord, have Thine
>   own way;
> Thou art the potter, I am the clay;
> Mold me and make me, after Thy will;
> While I am waiting, yielded and still.

When that becomes the sincere prayer of your heart, you, too, will become well content with weakness. And you will have taken another giant step toward advancing through adversity.

15

Responding to Adversity: The Choice Is Yours

We began in chapter 1 by looking at the possible sources of adversity. We found there were three: God, Satan, and sin. But it is not always easy to discern the source of our adversity. We have even seen cases in the Bible where they appear to overlap. It is evident that God's primary concern is not that we always understand the source of our adversity. Otherwise He would have made it clear. God is, however, extremely interested in how we respond to adversity because our response determines whether or not adversity is going to bring about its intended result.

The nature of our adversity alone does not determine its spiritual value in our lives. It is our reaction to it, the way we deal with it, that makes suffering valuable. We have all seen people who faced tough times and folded under the pressure. Some pull themselves back together and go on to learn whatever God wants to teach them. Others never recuperate.

The Blame Game

When adversity strikes, our first response oftentimes is to blame somebody. I can remember standing at the scene of an automobile accident listening to a college student trying to explain to the police officer why he had turned in front of a lady. He was sure that it was not his fault; something about the angle of the traffic light threw him off. He was clearly to blame. But this young man was so angry at having wrecked his car, he could not stand the thought of its being his fault.

We all have a tendency to strike out at those around us when things go wrong or we are hurt. Remember Mary and Martha's

256

But the man or
woman who has
God's perspective
on this life and
the life to come
will always emerge
victorious!

response: "Lord, if You had been here. . . ." Some people blame God. Others blame Satan. But usually we pin the blame on another person in an attempt to escape personal responsibility.

If blaming it on someone else does not get us anywhere, we may find ourselves fighting the problem. We attempt to manipulate or reshape our circumstances so as to rid ourselves of pain and inconvenience. This is the reason behind many lawsuits. People who have been fired or passed by for a promotion may sue the company. They feel impelled to fight for their rights.

Another way people react to tragedy is denial. They simply will not face what has happened. They act as if nothing is wrong. I see this in situations where someone has lost a loved one. And a parent or friend refuses to accept the separation as permanent. This is usually a temporary situation. In time, most of these people are able to accept what has happened.

Any of the preceding responses can easily turn into bitterness —bitterness toward the person or organization through which adversity comes or even bitterness toward God. When people become bitter, the very thought of the person who hurt them causes their stomach to turn. Bitterness forces people to over-react to circumstances that remind them of those through which they were wronged.

At this stage people may think about revenge. All of us are guilty at one time or another of rehearsing in our minds what we would like to do to somebody if we thought we could get away with it. We imagine ourselves walking into the office of our boss and letting him have it. Or perhaps calling our parents and telling them just what we think. Whatever the case, whenever there is a routine of imaginary confrontations, that is a good indication that bitterness has set in.

Bitterness toward God is much the same. A person who is bitter toward God cannot discuss religion objectively. There is always emotion involved. I have met a couple of self-proclaimed atheists who got so upset when the subject of God came up that they turned red! One would think that talking about something that did not exist would lend itself to an intellectually oriented discussion. But these people's atheism stemmed not from research and intellectual pursuits, but from hurt. At one time they had believed in God. But He did not act the way they thought He should, so they decided He did not exist. Such is the power of bitterness.

The Pity Party

Another common way of dealing with adversity is self-pity: "Oh my, what am I going to do? Nobody cares about me anymore. Look at my situation. I am hopeless. Before long I won't have any friends. I'll be alone. . . . Self-pity results from focusing exclusively on oneself rather than God. Individuals suffering from self-pity have drawn an imaginary circle around themselves and their circumstances. The only people they will allow in are those who want to join them in their misery. Consequently, they do oftentimes end up alone. No one wants to be around that type of person for long. This solitude serves to reinforce their negative perspective, and they cling to it even more tightly.

It is not unusual for these people to become depressed. Hopelessness overwhelms them, and they see no reason for going on with life. Depressed persons are unable to interpret accurately the events around them. Thus, if left alone, they tend to get worse.

Responding the wrong way to adversity will always have a devastating effect. People who react in any of the ways just described will always come out the losers. It is understandable why those who are hurt react the way they do. But regardless of how understandable their response may be, if it is a wrong response, they will suffer just the same.

Holding on to anger and bitterness is always self-destructive. Both are poisons. They poison your relationships, your decision-making ability, and your testimony. You cannot carry anger and bitterness and emerge from adversity a winner. Responding incorrectly to adversity only prolongs the agony. This is especially true if there is something specific God wants to teach you. He will not let up until He has accomplished His will.

There have been times when I felt as if I was on a Ferris wheel. Round and round I would go, experiencing the same hurt over and over again. "Lord," I would say, "what are You doing? I've already been through this." It was as if He said, "You're right, and when you respond correctly, I'll let you off."

God wants to use our pain and sorrow for something positive. When we respond incorrectly, we can rest assured He will devise another way to give us a second or third chance to handle it right.

In his book *Don't Waste Your Sorrows*, Paul

Billheimer states the same principle this way,

> Yielding to self-pity, depression, and rebellion is a waste of sorrow. Those who have unsuccessfully sought healing and who submit to resentment, discontent, impatience, and bitterness against God are wasting what God intended for growth in love and thus for enhanced rank in the eternal kingdom.

God intends to use adversity in our lives. That being the case, the wisest thing we can do is to learn to respond correctly. By doing so, we work with God rather than against Him.

The Right Response

I have divided this discussion into two parts. First, we will deal with how to respond to adversity that is the result of sin. Following that, we will focus on what our response should be when adversity originates with God or Satan.

The Wages of Sin

Sin always results in adversity of some form. Some types are certainly more obvious than others. And some are more devastating in their effect. But there is always a consequence of some sort, even if it is only guilt. The following are some steps I have found helpful in dealing with the consequences of sin.

1. Assume the Responsibility.

Don't look for someone else to blame. Don't think about what would have happened if someone had done something differently. Take the responsibility; own up to it. Admit to yourself that you are facing adverse circumstances because of your own doing.

2. Confess and Repent of Your Sin.

To confess is to agree with God. Tell God you have sinned. Not that you have made a mistake. Not that you have had an accident. Simply agree with Him that it is sin. Then repent of your sin. Make a decision not to return to it. That may entail ending a relationship. It may mean leaving your place of employment. You may have to go back to people you have wronged and apologize. Perhaps you have stolen from someone. Repentance would involve returning what you have taken. To repent is to make every arrangement necessary not to go back to the same sin. That way God knows you are serious.

3. Do Not Complain.

If you are suffering because of something you have done, you have no right to complain. You brought this on yourself. Don't spend your time trying to gain people's sympathy. Use your energy to get things right with God.

4. Ask God to Help You Discover the Weakness Through Which Sin Creeped into Your Life.

Is there a flaw in your thinking? Have you adopted ideas into your philosophy of life that are contrary to Scripture? Do you have an area of insecurity you have never dealt with? Do you have friends who drag you down? Is there someone in your life who is a constant source of temptation? Questions like these can help you pinpoint the door through which sin has entered and found a resting place in your life.

5. Recognize That God Wants to Use This Adversity in Your Life.

Regardless of the source, adversity is always a tool when entrusted to the hands of the Lord. Tell Him, "Lord, I know that I am suffering because of my own doing. But I trust that You will use this time of adversity to deepen my faith and strengthen my commitment to You."

6. Thank God for Not Allowing You to Get By with Your Sin.

True repentance is followed by genuine gratitude. When you see your sin for what it is and if you believe God disciplines those He loves, it makes sense to thank Him for sending adversity into your life if that is what it took to keep you from hurting yourself any further. No one enjoys adversity. But you can and should be grateful for what adversity accomplishes.

Adversity from Above and Below

Responding to adversity when it originates with God or Satan is different from merely responding to the consequences of sin. Yet, the way you respond when God is behind it and the way you respond when Satan is behind it is identical. This may come as a surprise. But think about it. Most of the time you really do not know who is behind it. And it really does not matter. What is important is your response.

Beyond that, however, another principle becomes a factor. You know if God is behind it, He is going to use it for your good. If Satan is behind it, you know he works under God's supervision. As you have seen in the life of Paul, God uses even Satan's schemes to accomplish His will. You are not pressed to discover the source, but you are expected to respond correctly.

You may think, But shouldn't I resist the devil? Shouldn't I stand against him with Scripture and prayer? Absolutely— when he comes at you with temptation. For you know that God has no part in tempting you. But we are not talking about temptation. The focus is adversity, unexpected tragedy, suffering. When these things occur, and you are sure it is not the direct result of your sin, here is how you should respond.

I. Reaffirm Your Position in Christ.

Remind yourself of who you are and what you have in Christ. It helps to do it aloud. You can say something like this:

> I know that I am a child of God. I am saved. I have been placed into Christ. I am sealed with the Holy Spirit. My eternal destiny is determined, and nothing can change that. The Lord will never leave me or forsake me. The angel of the Lord encampeth round about me. Nothing can touch me apart from what my loving heavenly Father allows. All things will work together for my good since I love God and have been called according to His purpose in Christ Jesus.

In his book, *God's New Creation*, Jack Taylor lists 365 statements of truth about the believer. He calls them "New Creation Confessions." They came to him in a moment of his life when he, too, was struggling with adversity. He writes,

> One day, far away from home and alone, I seemed to be enshrouded in a

cloud of anxiety, uncertainty, and depression. I could not pinpoint the exact source of my problem, but the feelings had to do with my real standing with God. The more I thought, the more exasperated I became. At last I spoke to God these words, "I would really love to know what you think of me." The Lord began to communicate with my troubled heart, urging me to go to the Word as if saying, "I have already made clear what I think of you in my Word. . . . read it!"

From that experience, Jack developed these 365 confessions. Truths such as these are essential to maintaining the right perspective on adversity. The reason is that self-esteem and confidence in God are usually the two things affected most by tragedy: "How could God allow this to happen to me?" In moments of despair you need a good strong dose of the truth to relieve your troubled heart.

2. Ask God to Remove the Adversity from Your Life.

This is usually where we begin. And I am sure the Lord understands. But it is best to ask after we have regained some perspective. Paul asked that his adversity be removed. God did not chastise him for that request. God will not be displeased by your request, either. Even your prayer for mercy is an expression of dependence and faith. God is always pleased when we demonstrate our faith.

3. Reaffirm the Promise of God's Sustaining Grace.

As we have seen, God may choose not to remove adversity from your life immediately. When that is the case, it is imperative that you rely on His grace rather than your own strength. People who try to endure suffering in their own strength go down under the weight of it all. Admit right up front that you do not have the power to withstand the pressure. Cry out to God for mercy. He will hear you. His grace will be sufficient moment by moment to get you through.

4. Thank God for This Unique Opportunity to Grow Spiritually.

You must look for God's part in your adversity, or you will miss it. You are not simply to endure suffering; you are to grow and mature through it. From the very outset you must look for the lessons God wants to teach you. The best way to develop this attitude is to thank Him every day for the spiritual growth He is bringing about in your life.

5. Receive Adversity as if It Were from God.

It does not matter if the adversity you are facing originated with Satan. Receive it as if it were from God. You know that nothing can happen to you unless He allows it. And if He allows it, He must certainly have a purpose in it. Therefore, as long as God is accomplishing His purpose through the adversity in your life, you can receive it as if it were from Him. When you respond to adversity as if it were from Satan, the tendency is to fight it. When it lingers, you may begin to doubt God.

I learned this principle during one of the most difficult periods of my life. After being at First Baptist Church for only a year, several deacons began a move to get me out of the church. As I prayed, I knew beyond any doubt that God wanted me to stay. Things got pretty rough for a while. People who I thought were my friends turned on me. I never knew where I stood from week to week.

On the one hand, I knew that if God wanted me to stay at FBC and they wanted me to leave, they certainly were not being led of the Spirit. That left only one option. Satan was clearly behind the controversy. Yet on the other, I knew that somehow the Lord was in it as well. One day I was in my office praying, and a thought came to me that I know now was from the Lord: The only way to deal with this is not to took at men, but to keep your eyes on Me. It doesn't matter who says what, when, where, or how. You must see all this as coming from Me.

From that moment on, I began thanking God for what He was doing. Things got worse before they got better. But God was faithful. He accomplished many great things through that time—both in my life and in the life of the church. In spite of all the rejection and deception, I never grew bitter. To this day I am not resentful. The thing that got me through it was trusting that somehow God was in it and that when He had accomplished His purpose, things would change. In the meantime my responsibility was to remain faithful.

As long as you are able to believe that God is involved in the adversity you are facing, you will have hope. Regardless of who initiated it, God is in it! And if He is in it, His grace for you will be sufficient. It does not make any difference who the source is. It matters very little who the messenger is. As long as you respond as if it were from God, you will come out a winner.

6. Read and Meditate on Scriptures Describing the Adversities of God's Servants.

Read the story of Joseph. Put yourself in the place of Moses when he was told he could not enter the Promised Land. Look at the way God provided for Abraham when he was left with the least desirable land. Imagine how foolish Noah felt while building the ark. The Bible contains illustration after illustration of God's faithfulness in adverse circumstances. Fill your mind with these truths. Ask Him to open your eyes to the human side of these characters that you might be able to identify with their pain and their sorrow. Then dwell on Christ's promise to care for those who love Him (see Matt. 6:25–34). Just as He was faithful to those whose stories are in the Old and New Testaments, so will He demonstrate His faithfulness to you.

A Final Word

Suffering is unavoidable. It comes without warning; it takes us by surprise. It can shatter or strengthen us. It can be the source of great bitterness or abounding joy. It can be the means by which our faith is destroyed. Or it can be the tool through which our faith is deepened. The outcome hinges not on the nature or source of our adversity, but on the character and spirit of our response. Our response to adversity will for the most part be determined by our reason for living, our purpose for being on this earth, as we see it.

If you are a child of God whose heart's desire is to see God glorified through you, adversity will not put you down for the count. There will be those initial moments of shock and confusion. But the man or woman who has God's perspective on this life and the life to come will always emerge victorious!

Walker and Company Large Print books are available at your local bookstore.
Please ask for them.
If you want to receive a catalog of our titles, send your name and address to:

Beth Walker
Walker and Company
435 Hudson Street
New York, New York 10014

Look for these latest Walker Large Prints

Footprints
Margaret Fishback Powers

Just As I Am
Billy Graham

Keep a Quiet Heart
Elisabeth Elliot

The Lady, Her Lover, and Her Lord
T. D. Jakes

A Layman Looks At the Lord's Prayer
W. Phillip Keller

Letters to My Grandchildren
Charlie W. Shedd

Readings for Meditation and Reflection
C. S. Lewis

Stories for the Heart
Alice Gray

Among the many other titles available are:

Abiding In Christ
Cynthia Heald

And the Angels Were Silent
Max Lucado

Apples of Gold
Jo Petty

The Best of Catherine Marshall
edited by Leonard LeSourd

The Blood
Benny Hinn

A Book of Angels
Sophy Burnham

Book of Hours
Elizabeth Yates

Breakfast with Billy Graham

Brush of an Angel's Wing
Charlie W. Shedd

Encourage Me
Charles Swindoll

15 Minutes Alone with God
Emilie Barnes

Finding God
Larry Crabb

Finding God in Unexpected Places
Philip Yancey

A Gathering of Hope
Helen Hayes

Getting Through the Night
Eugenia Price

God Came Near
Max Lucado

Golden Treasury of Psalms and Prayers
Edna Beilenson

Good Morning, Holy Spirit
Benny Hinn

The Grace Awakening
Charles Swindoll

The Greatest Salesman in the World
Og Mandino

The Greatest Story Ever Told
Fulton Oursler